SEXUAL WHOLENESS
in Marriage

An LDS Perspective on Integrating
Sexuality and Spirituality in our Marriages

DEAN M. BUSBY, Ph.D.

JASON S. CARROLL, Ph.D.

CHELOM LEAVITT, J.D., M.S.

Sexual Wholeness in Marriage:
An LDS Perspective on Integrating Sexuality and Spirituality in our Marriages

Contact: dean_busby@byu.edu
ISBN 978-0-9819576-4-7

Cover design by Barry Hansen Creative
Text layout by Book Printers of Utah, Inc.

ACKNOWLEDGEMENTS

To our spouses: We understand more than most the trials you have to endure by being married to "relationship experts." Each chapter, each paragraph, and nearly each sentence reminds us of how we hope to be more consistently the spouses you deserve. It is a testament to the power of love that you stay with us in spite of our duplicity. You continue to teach us the deeper meanings of the word *intimacy*.

To our children: Even though we once thought that we were raising you, with maturity—and some astonishment—we have come to realize that you are angels sent to deliver God's grace in our lives. You, the fruit of our intimacy, have truly become "sweet above all that is sweet." It is our simple prayer that some small portion of this book may help you and your spouses on your journey toward oneness.

ABOUT THE AUTHORS

Dean M. Busby, Ph.D. is director of the School of Family Life at Brigham Young University in Provo, Utah. He received his doctorate in Family Therapy from Brigham Young University, after which he taught at Syracuse University and Texas Tech University where he was department chair. He has published numerous books, book chapters, and research articles in the area of marriage relationships, sexuality, relationship education and intervention, assessment of couples, and relationship trauma. His research has garnered university and national awards and funding by federal and state grants. Dr. Busby has taught at the university level for over 20 years primarily in the area of dating and marriage relationships, family violence, and research methods, and his courses are popular and well-received. He and his wife Colleen have been married 30 years and are the parents of three sons.

Jason S. Carroll, Ph.D. is associate director of the School of Family Life at Brigham Young University in Provo, Utah. He received his doctorate from the Department of Family Social Science at the University of Minnesota. Dr. Carroll is a nationally recognized researcher, scholar, and educator in the areas of marriage readiness among young adults, couple formation patterns and the transition to marriage, the effectiveness of marriage education, and modern threats to marriage such as materialism, pornography, delayed age at marriage, and premarital sexuality. He is also lead instructor of the *Preparation for Marriage* course at BYU which services nearly 1,500 students annually. As an educator, Dr. Carroll consistently receives high evaluations from students for his thought-provoking and substantive classes. A highly sought-after public speaker, his writings have been featured in *USA Today, Psychology Today, The Wall Street Journal, NPR, GQ, Glamour, Elle, Focus on the Family*, and other media outlets. He and his wife Stefani have been married 20 years and are the parents of five children.

Chelom Leavitt, J.D., M.S. is a practicing lawyer and marriage and parenting educator. She received her juris doctor in 1992 and has specialized in family legal issues since her admission to the Utah State Bar that same year. From 2004 to the present, she has directed an international legal institute which teaches law in 18 Ukrainian law schools, five Moldovan law schools, and the governmental legal institute in Rwanda. In 2010 Chelom received her M.S. degree from Brigham Young University in Marriage, Family and Human Development. She was also selected by the U.S. State Department to receive the prestigious Fulbright Fellowship in Ukraine for psychology as a result of her marriage and family studies at BYU. As a Fulbright Fellow in Ukraine, she taught courses at the Kiev Taras Shevchenko National University on marriage and parenting. Chelom and her husband David have been married 23 years and are the parents of seven children.

TABLE OF CONTENTS

FOREWORD

As colleagues who have worked together for many years, we frequently talk about experiences we have with students while teaching courses on dating, court-ship, and marriage. In recent years our conversations have often focused on our experiences while teaching the subject of sexuality to Latter-day Saint young adults and couples. We have discussed what we might do to help them be better prepared to have more fulfilling experiences in this sensitive area in their relationships. Why do questions about sexuality seem to come up more often than they used to in our classes? Is there some new factor in students' lives, or in their backgrounds, or in the media they use that is creating more problems for them on this issue? We have wondered whether we should refer them to a certain book or other resource that might teach them more thoroughly than could our class lessons or private visits?

Unfortunately, after reviewing the existing LDS and other Christian-oriented books on sexuality in marriage, and even after having referred people to some of them over the years, we have concluded that each book seems to be lacking at least some of the central material that could be the most helpful to this group.

Furthermore, after we searched through the more secular writings on this topic, we are even less comfortable referring people to these sources; the information is often more detailed, but the lack of values reflected in such sources leads them to suggest "solutions" that to us are neither appropriate nor effective. In short, such secular books and websites are more likely to create new problems for couples than resolve existing concerns.

Consequently, we considered the possibility of writing a new book on healthy sexuality and marital intimacy. Yet even with the persistent concerns expressed by our students, and the sense that the available literature was not as helpful as we wanted, we were still hesitant. Even though we are practicing marriage educators, marriage scholars, and college teachers where sexual issues are regularly addressed, none of us has had an agenda to write such a book. We were each reluctant to give advice about a topic that to us is so very sacred, yet is so often reduced to tawdry sensationalism by most others in our modern society. Besides, does our world really need another book about sex? We have repeatedly asked ourselves this question. The fact that you are now reading this foreword declares that we finally answered that question in the affirmative.

A Book for the Latter-days

Several recent trends have helped us overcome our reluctance to write an LDS-oriented book on healthy sexuality and marital intimacy. For many years we have each given presentations about the topic of marriage to audiences, many of whom were conservative and Christian. We typically invite the audience to write down questions, confidentially, about their marriage relationships that have gone unanswered. Inevitably, most of these questions are about sexuality. This is not necessarily surprising since the topic of sexuality is so difficult to talk about for so many people. What has been surprising, though, is the degree of anxiety, frustration, ignorance, and confusion that is often embedded in those questions.

When the setting is conducive to openly discuss this topic, it becomes even more obvious that challenges with sexuality are very common. We have had confirmed through these questions and other discussions that many otherwise stable couples are starting out their marriages on a shaky footing in the sexuality area.

Ironically, even though we are surrounded by almost an ocean of sexual information—more than any prior generation—we are not necessarily more wise about how to successfully manage this key area of married life and confidently discuss it with our spouses. If anything, couples seem more confused and less successful in this facet of their relationships than those of earlier generations. *Why is this the case?* we ask.

One of the answers to this question has to do with another recent mega-trend in our lives, one that is on the same scale as when our culture shifted from an agricultural to an industrial-based society. Many of us are virtually connected to the internet and other people 24 hours a day, and we are swimming in more information than anyone from any period of earth's history. In fact, recent studies suggest that our youth are in front of a screen (smart phone, computer, or television) during almost every waking hour of their lives. Many of them even carry the internet into their beds at night for more texting, tweeting, and blogging.

Such constant connectedness to information and to other people through technology has become as common in our lives as the air we breathe.

But how do these trends affect sexuality? Most will agree that sex is one of the more alluring and interesting topics in life. That interest, combined with easy access to nearly unlimited information—accurate or not—creates an environment where much of our discussions and much of the information we access is going to be about sex.

This is especially so when access is more available at younger and younger ages with little parental supervision. Hence we may "know" more about the topic of sex because of the amount of information we have read, heard, or watched. Nevertheless, most of us did not get clear and timely instructions from our parents and other trustworthy people that could have helped us distinguish truth from error, and teach us how to successfully navigate this crucial area of our lives.

Youth tend to seek additional information about their bodies and sexuality from friends, books, and sources other than parents and local church authorities, as we informants are mostly silent on the specifics of this intriguing topic, except to say that it is sacred and something that should wait until marriage.

In fact, recent research confirms that this pattern began decades ago; research also shows that religious parents are less likely to discuss sex with their children than non-religious parents. What is different today is that the amount of information available from sources other than parents and churches is exponentially larger, while the amount of information shared by parents and church sources has remained relatively constant.

Consider the figure on the following page.

What has been the effect of the growth of information from sources that may not be trustworthy? What are the values of the people who are providing this ever expanding information about sex?

Many of our students tell us that if they heard anything at all from their parents about sex it was usually during a very uncomfortable "talk" somewhere around the age of puberty. Despite encouragement from church authorities for parents to discuss sexual matters openly and often with their children, many parents are still

Amount of Sexual Information Learned from Different Sources

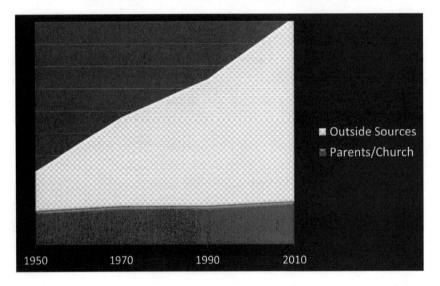

not adequately doing this. Our students say that what they generally learned from parents and local church authorities are rules about what should not be done; they weren't taught how to understand, manage, and appropriately express their feelings about their bodies and desires.

Even when we turn to the written sources about sexuality from acceptable outlets, we find that LDS and other Christian sources tend to be vague rather than specific, and focus on medical and spiritual aspects of the topic.

Such sources are better than nothing, but a more direct approach may prove to be more beneficial. A more straightforward approach that includes solid scientific research on the attachment and complex emotions associated with sex, and one that also addresses the common questions that couples have about sexuality, may finally help couples reduce the confusion about their sexual lives.

Discussing Sexuality: Not a Matter of *If*, But a Matter of *Whom*

A number of years ago we were asked to present a lesson about sexuality as part of the ward conferences in a stake. A particularly wise stake president was concerned about the number of people with sexual issues with whom he and his bishops were counseling. So we led an hour-long discussion on the topic in each ward.

After we had given a few of these presentations, word got around to the other wards about "the topic" that would be addressed in the adult session of the ward conferences. Before one of the presentations we happened to overhear two women in the foyer who were talking about our upcoming class:

So did you hear what we are going to be talking about next?

 No, what?

Sex.

 Ughh.

I know. I don't know why we have to talk about that stuff at church.

It is unlikely that their attitude is unique. Not too many years later, one of us, while serving as a bishop's counselor, was asked by our bishop to speak in sacrament meeting. The bishop had heard one of us speak on BYU-TV at Womens Conference on marriage relationships and asked if that same talk could be given in our ward. Even though this talk was being broadcast regularly on BYU-TV, one ward member was offended by this sacrament service talk that used the phrase "marital intimacy," and which counseled spouses to be *other-centered* in such "expressions of love." An anonymous letter was soon received by both the bishop and stake president expressing these concerns and calling for the speaker's release from the bishopric.

These experiences suggest that some people still continue to believe that sexuality and marital intimacy should not be discussed in any church meetings, meetings that can affect our progress toward salvation. Of course careful consideration needs to be given in settings where young children are present; but such attitudes often still exist when the audience is made up of teens, young adults, or married couples.

Such attitudes tend to perpetuate negative views regarding our physical bodies and our God-given desires for intimacy, and send subtle messages that these facets of our being are inappropriate or evil. These experiences also suggest that some people have a naïve understanding about the modern environment surrounding their families and children, and that they themselves are not openly and regularly discussing this important topic.

A recent study supports this concern: it found that most parents think their teenage children are not as interested in sex as are other youth; that rarely, if ever, do the parents know about the sexual attitudes, behaviors, and difficulties of their own children; that the parents assume their children don't have any difficulties! There is no better way to counteract the inaccurate and destructive messages about sexuality we are receiving than to clearly and consistently discuss this key aspect of our mortal lives.

Like the Book of Mormon prophet, Jacob, we would prefer to not risk offending anyone's sensitive nature by discussing such things so openly and directly in a public setting. But we live in a world with real challenges. There seems to be no topic that is given more attention in our media, and no dimension of discipleship where the adversary is applying more pressures on us than the area of sexuality.

In the last days of the Nephite people, both Mormon and Moroni would have preferred to live in a time of peace—yet constant carnage and bloodshed surrounded them. Alas, their lot was to live at the time they lived, so they committed themselves to "labor diligently" (Moroni 9: 6) to help people survive spiritually in a time of gross warfare.

Likewise, we would prefer to not live in the current climate of spiritual warfare that centers around our sexual attitudes and behaviors. Wouldn't it be wonderful to live in a world where everyone was faithful to their spouses; where no one became involved in pornography; where no immodest images were used to advertise everything from hamburgers to domain websites; where we did not have to worry about sexually transmitted diseases and unmarried pregnant teenagers; where we did not have to fret that our children were going to be accosted by sexual messages every day?

Alas, we do not live in such a day, so let us also "labor diligently" to positively influence this important aspect of our lives.

Fortunately, our future can be brighter than that of the Nephites. Latter-day Saints can press forward with the assurance that those who are striving to live virtuous lives and strictly keep their covenants with God will not be overcome by evil; they can build Zion-like homes, wards, and stakes—even in a season of broad spiritual darkness.

There is much to be hopeful about. And when we do not live up to our ideals, we understand the process of change, the power of the atonement of Jesus Christ, and can recover our purity. When we have a clear understanding of the gospel, and a clear understanding of the principles of intimacy, we can then celebrate our sexuality in wholesome and divinely-designed ways.

SECTION I

INTRODUCTION

1

FREQUENT QUESTIONS & COMMON MISUNDERSTANDINGS

In our work as university professors, marriage educators, and couple therapists, we have interacted with thousands of students and hundreds of couples in church-related presentations, community seminars, firesides, and private counseling sessions. In each of these settings we are nearly always asked questions—sometimes in front of the class, and other times after class or in a private setting. Let us introduce you to a few examples.

While we are not sure exactly how common these situations are, nevertheless the types of questions they contain and the experiences they describe have been echoed in enough questions over the years to where we feel comfortable using them to introduce many of the issues we will be addressing in this book.

Jenny

Jenny came up at the end of a class on marital conflict while her professor was gathering up his materials. She was obviously struggling to muster the courage to ask a question, so her professor invited her to meet in a more private setting where she could ask her question.

> *My husband and I have been married for about a year. He likes to have sex every day, but I'm getting a little worn out by it all, and sometimes I don't want sex at all for many days. Is there something wrong with me?*

> *He thinks that if we get one of those sex manuals and figure out some different positions or something, it might become more interesting to me. What do you think?*

While it may be tempting to answer Jenny's sincere question by giving the short answer that it is normal for husbands and wives to have different levels of interest in sex—and no information in any book was going to change that, as is often the case, there were patterns in Jenny's relationship with her husband that make this seemingly simple question more complicated. As instructors and therapists, we learned years ago that when a conservative Christian like Jenny asks a question about sexuality, it usually means there is something much more challenging than the original issue that needs to be addressed.

In the course of the conversation Jenny explained that she and her husband, Steve, met about six months before their wedding, fell in love quickly, got engaged a few months later, and married in the summer between their junior and senior years of college. Jenny said that while she was—and still is—attracted to her husband, it was clear to her from the beginning of their relationship that he was much more interested in sex than she was. While they were both virgins when they married, during their dating months he was usually pushing for more passionate levels of kissing than she was comfortable with, so she usually set the boundaries to which he reluctantly complied. They spent the first few weeks of their courtship talking intensely and really felt like their relationship "just clicked."

Soon after Jenny and Steve began to be exclusive, however, they talked less and their dating relationship turned more physical when most of the evenings they spent together ended up as make-out sessions. Sometimes Jenny would say she wanted to "slow things down"—and they would for a few days; but eventually their time together would again turn more physical. Originally Jenny and Steve were planning to marry in December, but as things got "more steamy" they moved their plans up to July. Even then they had to "stay away from each other" during the last few weeks of their engagement to avoid "getting into trouble."

Jenny said that during their honeymoon and early months of marriage she enjoyed sex and found it all wonderful and exciting; but she noticed that even during those initial months of her marriage that she wasn't as interested in sex as Steve was. She said that after about six months of sex almost every day—and some-times more than once a day—she just started to lose interest entirely. She began to withhold affection from Steve, and would try to avoid any physical contact that might get him interested in having sex. The only time she felt totally free to hold hands or engage in other types of mild physical contact was at church where she knew it "wouldn't lead to something else."

Recently Jenny was beginning to worry that all Steve really cared about was sex, and not about connecting with her as a whole person. She resented him for that, and felt like their sexual patterns were pushing them apart rather than bringing them together. When she was asked if she had ever talked to her husband about these feelings, she mentioned two examples that were typical of their communication about sex. Earlier in their marriage when she would say something like, "Let's do something else tonight rather than just have sex," Steve would reply, "Just have sex! What could be better than sex?!" She would always feel bad after such conversations, as if there was something wrong with her for not wanting sex very often.

Jenny's second example was when she would become so frustrated that they rarely did anything together other than sex. Jenny would then ignore most of Steve's efforts to initiate intimacy, and she would eventually refuse flat out to have sex; Steve would pout for as long as it took to wear her down. Recently, she had just resigned herself to the way it was and she would give in most evenings. But Steve seemed to notice her lack of interest, so that is why he had suggested getting a book that could help them find ways to spice things up, so she might enjoy sex more. She freely added that she didn't think sex itself was bad, but recently she was turned off by the idea altogether. It just took too long to get into the mood, so she would just fake it to get through it sooner.

Alex

Alex was in the tenth year of his marriage when he attended a talk about how to protect your marriage from divorce. After the talk he sent a note to the presenter describing his concerns.

> *Dear Dr—, I really enjoyed your talk last night and wanted to ask you a question. In regard to sexuality, you mentioned that some scholars consider this part of marriage to be one of the best gauges of the overall health of the relationship. That struck me because I think my wife and I have some challenges that worry me. Don't get me wrong, we love each other and are committed to our relationship, but sometimes it is so*

confusing knowing what to do in the sexual area. She is more comfortable with her body and with talking about sex, and I am very shy about these things.

Sometimes I think it is because she was a nonmember until she was 22 and had sexual experiences before her baptism, while I have been a member all my life and have never had sex with anyone but her. So I'm not sure she has the proper attitude about these things and I worry that we are doing things that are wrong. She says I'm just too hung up about being perfect, and God gave us these bodies to enjoy so I should lighten up. I don't know what to think. I mean she is an amazing woman and all, but I'm not sure she is as spiritually in tune as she should be.

Anyway, she usually likes to enjoy things sexually other than intercourse, and she says they help her climax better, but I think intercourse is better and the proper way. Isn't intercourse the natural and normal way to have sex and other ways are perversions?

Shannon

Shannon was enrolled in a course that dealt with current research about marriage. During the early part of the semester they read about research on what was called attachment styles, and discussed how people who had parents who were emotionally unavailable when they were young are more likely to have adult attachment styles characterized by anxiety or avoidance. When her professor described how an adult with an anxious attachment style commonly acted, Shannon definitely saw herself in the description. She recognized that she had felt so insecure in the early years of their marriage that it was a miracle her husband, David, had stayed with her.

She recalled an experience where she had been looking through some of the websites he had visited and noticed one that contained suggestive pictures and content. She was devastated for weeks about this, and when she finally mentioned it to David he blew up, accusing her of "checking up on him like he was a little kid." She immediately apologized and they never talked about it again. She worried that she was again becoming overly anxious and insecure, worried that her husband may have a problem with pornography and had turned to it because she wasn't a good enough wife or lover. She wrote the following question to her instructor after the course ended.

> *I really loved your class and wanted to ask you a question. I learned that I have an anxious attachment style, so I generally feel insecure in my relationships and need a lot of reassurances. So maybe I'm making a mountain out of a molehill, but a few months ago I found that my husband had visited a pornographic site. He blew up when he found out I was checking up on him and we haven't talked about it since. Last week I checked again and it doesn't look like he has visited any more sites like that, but maybe since he knew I was checking he is just deleting his internet history file.*
>
> *I don't want to be so insecure where I feel I have to check up on my husband, but isn't pornography a hard habit to break? Do men look at these things because they are unhappy in their marriage? I don't know if we can talk about this without it causing a bad argument, but I can't seem to let it go. What should I do?*

Joshua

Joshua attended a workshop on marriage enrichment hoping to gain knowledge and develop skills he could use in his future career as a therapist. During the section of the workshop that focused on improving marital intimacy, he was shocked to learn that nearly 40% of women have a difficult time reaching orgasm through sexual intercourse alone, and that wives usually take at least four times longer to reach orgasm than their husbands. He also learned that the definition of premature ejaculation fit his situation. So when he considered his own marriage, he felt badly for his wife and upset that he hadn't learned such information earlier so that he could have helped make sex more enjoyable for her. He wrote the following to the workshop leader during an exercise where participants were encouraged to write down any question they wanted on a 3 x 5 card that was then turned in confidentially.

> *When I learned about how much more complicated sexual enjoyment can be for women than men, I felt bad that I had been ignorant of this information for so long in our marriage. I also learned that I have a*

problem with premature ejaculation, when I assumed everything was normal. My wife is kind about these things and would never want me to feel bad about my performance, but I'm sure she hasn't enjoyed sex as much as she could have. I'm frustrated that nobody provided this vital information to me before we married. Maybe I should have asked her, but I just assumed she was more like me; I didn't realize how different men and women were in their needs.

Why don't we teach people about these specific issues in some premarital class or something so more couples avoid having less satisfying experiences than they otherwise might have? How can we learn to talk about these things as a couple and as parents so that our relationships can improve, and so our children won't have to suffer from the same ignorance we suffered from?

Responding to the Questions

When we are approached by people who are having challenges in their dating and marriage relationships, we experience a variety of thoughts and feelings. But above all, we want to help them find sound answers to their vexing questions so that their relationships and marriages can improve, rather than struggle or develop worse problems. In Jenny's situation, we suspect that if something doesn't change she is going to become increasing fatigued about sex and may find it more and more aversive. She may eventually become so resentful of sex that she avoids her husband, such that the strong commitment she has for her marriage begins to weaken.

It is important to note that we lack her husband Steve's perspective on these issues; he may already be frustrated and distressed as well. What will he do if sex becomes less frequent and thus less fulfilling for him in his marriage? Will he continue to view his wife as the one who is responsible for the problem? Or will he have the maturity to consider that his own attitudes and expectations may be causing some of their challenges? Furthermore, has he developed the skills to communicate and negotiate with his wife so that they can mutually agree to broaden their relationship beyond just the physical? What seems to be keeping this couple from talking about these issues more openly with one another?

Over the years, we have found that sexuality is a major stumbling block for many couples who are trying to form a loving and lasting marriage. In fact, we have come to believe that without some assistance, many couples may struggle needlessly during courtship and early marriage, with some eventually heading toward divorce. We are also persuaded that these types of questions are being asked more frequently by a growing percentage of our people.

The Need for a Model of Sexual Wholeness

In this book we will present and then answer the most common questions that emerge when we teach and present on the topics of sexuality. We will attempt to address many more questions beyond the few presented in this chapter, but we hope you can appreciate that these questions are complex and multi-faceted. Some may indicate a lack of knowledge about general sexual functioning, while others seem to be a signal of deeper emotional challenges. Some questions are about relationship aspects of sexuality, and others are more about specific sexual anatomy and physical functioning.

Let's say, for example, that we are trying to answer Joshua's question about finding a way to more openly talk about sex with his wife. There are some simple and specific approaches that we could share that might help him and his wife have better experiences and learn to talk more openly. However, what we do not know are some of the important nuances about this problem for this particular couple.

Maybe they aren't able to openly talk about sexuality in their relationship because one partner had traumatic sexual experience as a child and they now find it distressing to even think about sex. Or maybe one of them strongly prefers to avoid discussing any topic that might create tension or conflict. You can see how knowing the origin or root cause of their difficulties is key to understanding how to appropriately address their questions, so that the advice will be truly helpful. Therefore, simply answering questions without such a comprehensive perspective of sexuality has the potential to create more problems than it solves.

Books and websites about sex typically provide so little specificity about how to deal with problems that they are not very useful. Some books discuss practices and techniques, but are not grounded in the spiritual and emotional aspects of sexuality—aspects that are vital for determining whether a particular approach will be helpful. We see then that to effectively answer specific questions we need to first provide a correct model of sexual wholeness. As we answer specific questions later in the book, we will refer to this model often without repeating its general principles for each question we answer.

What are the key components of a model of sexual wholeness? According to the readings, research, and professional experience we have with this topic, there are at least three primary dimensions of human sexuality. While these three dimensions are intricately intertwined, it is useful to distinguish them from each other because different types of problems and questions can emerge from each dimension.

The first dimension that helps us understand the meaning and purpose of sex is the spiritual dimension. It would be inappropriate to answer specific questions about sexuality unless we first understand why sex exists, and how it fits into the broader plan about the purpose of life. To become sexually whole we need to become spiritually whole.

The second dimension is the physical dimension. This area tends to receive the most attention in terms of scientific research. We know much about how the brain, our hormones, and our genes work together to create the physical part of our sexual nature. To become whole sexually we should clearly understand our physical bodies, and how our bodies influence—and are influenced by—the other two dimensions of our sexual nature.

The third dimension of our model of sexual wholeness is the emotional dimension. Our sexual behaviors occur within relationships we have with other people. The quality of our relationship significantly influences our sexual quality, and our sexual quality significantly influences the quality of our relationship. Most of us feel a strong need to be close to at least some people in our lives. Such emotional cravings are every bit as strong as the physical appetites connected to sex.

Our various experiences of attachment significantly influence how we express our sexuality and maintain our relationships. Some of the greatest joys we may experience as spouses are linked to the opportunity to unselfishly respond to each other in the intimacy of marriage. Some insightful experts have even argued that the sexual quality of our relationship is the clearest indicator of how well our overall marital relationship is functioning. To be sexually whole we should do much more than learn specific physical techniques to arouse our bodies; we should seek to experience our sexuality within a strong committed relationship—one where we have the safety to openly explore this symbolic area of life together in ways that will help us become one.

The absence of this model of sexual integration and wholeness appears to be the most glaring omission in the existing information available to couples. We have found that after we articulate this model, most couples are able to answer their own questions. Couples can apply the general principles of this model to effectively address specific questions about sexuality in a variety of areas in their relationship that include sexual norms across the lifespan; choosing sexual behaviors within marriage; and proper patterns of sexual expression during dating and courtship. Within each of these areas and others, we will attempt to answer common questions we have encountered.

Why a Principle-based Approach?

We want to emphasize that as we discuss marital sexuality, our focus will be on broad principles of sexuality, rather than specific sexual practices or techniques. There are three reasons why we will use a principle-based approach:

First, principles are what matter most. One of the great myths in our popular culture is that sexual fulfillment in a couple's relationship is mostly the result of using proper techniques. While a proper understanding of men's and women's bodies—as well as human sexual response patterns—can be helpful in fostering pleasurable sexual experiences, lasting sexual fulfillment is primarily about the quality of your entire relationship with your spouse—something our pop culture tends to ignore. The principles we discuss in this book are designed to teach us how to have a fulfilling sexual relationship, not just stimulating pleasurable sexual responses.

The second reason we will focus on principles rather than practices is that patterns of satisfying sex vary from couple to couple; as such, the only couple you need to be familiar with when it comes to the specifics of sex is your own marriage. Therefore, your sexual relationship in marriage needs to be tailored to you and your spouse—not to outside expectations or comparisons.

The third and perhaps most important reason for focusing on principles with this topic is that some parts of marital sexuality are only meant to be learned together as a couple. This book is designed to foster that; it will provide a foundation upon which to build as you explore and discover a fullness of sexuality and intimacy in your marriage. The Lord intended for it to be this way, and He knows best how to guide you toward deep sexual fulfillment and true intimacy.

We hope this approach will open up authentic conversations between spouses, conversations that will help them establish their own unique shared patterns that can enhance their intimacy and oneness with each other.

Conclusion

What about Jenny, Alex, Shannon, and Joshua? How were their questions answered, and what happened in their relationships? We will discuss each of their relationships again as we describe more specifics of the model of sexual wholeness. We will use the experiences of their marriages to illustrate how the model can help couples answer their own questions that emerge in the sexual area. By the end of the book, we hope their experiences will help you better understand some of the challenges you may face with sexuality, and teach you how you can find the answers you need on your road to sexual wholeness.

Questions to Ponder

Consider each question yourself, then use them to prompt a discussion with your spouse.

1. *How do I show that I am comfortable with my own body?*
2. *How do I show that I consider my physical body as a gift from God?*
3. *What does intimacy mean to me?*
4. *How have I developed (or ignored) the spiritual area of sexual wholeness?*
5. *How have I developed (or ignored) the emotional area of sexual wholeness?*
6. *How have I developed (or ignored) the physical area of sexual wholeness?*

2

BEYOND ABSTINENCE:
FINDING A NEW SEXUAL METAPHOR

Many people have built collections of various types. Some people like to collect stamps, others collect coins, and some collect spoons. As marriage educators and researchers we have acquired a collection as well, but ours is different than most; ours is a collection of hundreds of personal stories from church members explaining how they were taught about sexuality. We asked our students and others to share with us how and what they learned about this topic while growing up, and we have carefully accumulated their verbal and written stories.

These very personal accounts provide a unique window into the sexual culture of many LDS homes and wards. We are particularly intrigued by how frequently we are told by young people that their parents and church leaders used object lessons to teach them about sexuality. These lessons are highly symbolic and tend to compare sex to an object or to a pattern of behavior. Much can be learned from understanding the metaphors and messages that are intentionally—and unintentionally—expressed. Nearly all such object lessons we have been told about can be grouped into two categories: 1) fear-based metaphors, and 2) abstinence-based metaphors. So as we tell you about these personal accounts, reflect on your own experiences in learning about sexuality. Is your experience similar to any of those we describe?

Fear-Based Metaphors

The "fear-based metaphor" label is not meant to imply that the parents, ward leaders, or seminary teachers who have used these metaphors were trying to frighten their young learners. In fact, we are confident that the individuals who used this type of object lesson were well-intending people, who were just trying to impress an important concept upon the minds of their children or class members. Nevertheless, and in spite of the good intentions of the teachers, such lessons caused most of the "students" to have feelings of fear and anxiety, and other unintended negative messages about sexuality.

Fear-based metaphors typically compare sex to something being damaged or being made unclean. For example, a seminary teacher once showed a class a delicious wrapped cupcake and asked if any of them would like to eat it. After many students enthusiastically said they wanted the treat, the teacher then unwrapped the cupcake and had them pass it around. After each person had handled it, the seminary teacher then asked, *Who would like to eat the cupcake now?* Of course the point of the lesson was clear: the cupcake had become unclean and undesirable. The instructor then compared the "handled" cupcake with the impurity of sexual involvement before marriage.

Another version of this type of object lesson uses chewing gum as the metaphor. In yet another flowers were used, where after all of the class members had touched the delicate petals they would soon wilt and turn brown. Again, the parallel was then drawn that such inappropriate "touching" spoiled a beautiful thing, leaving it wilted and damaged.

Another young woman told us about an object lesson that was used at a Girl's Camp where leaders wanted to teach the young women about the importance of sexual purity before marriage. As they gathered around the fire (a genuine fireside!), a beautiful white wedding dress was brought out and held up as a symbol of being clean and pure on one's wedding day. During the lesson, however, as examples of immodest and unworthy behaviors were discussed, portions of the dress were then cut out and thrown into the campfire.

Perhaps the most dramatic fear-based object lesson we have been told about occurred in a young women's lesson where the leader was comparing personal purity to a beautiful china plate. As she showed the girls the plate, she admired its beauty and fine craftsmanship. She extolled its uniqueness and noted that it was worth a very high price. Then without warning, the leader turned and threw the plate against the wall, shattering it into pieces! The girls were then told that to be sexually impure before marriage was similar to throwing their "purity plate" against a wall—thus devaluing something of great worth.

Now, not all fear-based metaphors involve shattering plates, burning wedding dresses, or soiling food. A more typical form of fear-based teaching about sexuality is seen in the awkward conveyance of the message rather than the content. Many young people have told us about finding a copy of a "chastity talk" under their pillow when they went to bed, or other materials their parents had left for them to read rather than discussing the topic face-to-face. Some have told us of parents who would become so uncomfortable during conversations about sexuality that they would change the topic whenever it came up. Others have related that their parents had one "big talk" with them about the "birds and the bees," and didn't bring it up again.

We have also been told that some LDS parents follow a strict gender pattern for conversations about sexuality where moms are the only parent to talk to daughters, and dads are the only parent to talk to sons. Time and again, teens and young adults in the church tell us that their parents and many of their leaders seemed nervous and very uncomfortable while trying to discuss the topic of sex in a direct and meaningful manner.

Associated with fear-based metaphors, many Latter-day Saints report that the only discussion they have had about sexuality is when they were taught the evils of pornography and sexual transgression. If, however, such counsel does not include positive views of marital intimacy and healthy sexuality, the unintended message may be internalized that pornography is sex, and thus sex is pornography. Many people struggle to differentiate between healthy sexual desires and the temptations of pornography, as well as what constitutes a "pornography problem" versus the normal process of sexual maturation from youth to young adulthood. Too often, negative emotions and legitimate concerns associated with pornography and sexual transgression become fused with and overshadow understandings about sex.

A Negative Portrayal of Sexual Intimacy

One of the primary consequences of fear-based object lessons and metaphors about sexuality is a negative portrayal of sexual intimacy, often unintentionally conveying to young minds that sex is a bad thing that harms us. While sexual sin clearly has negative effects on our lives, fear-based object lessons typically don't include a balanced discussion about the positive consequences associated with healthy sexuality. Even when a balanced view of sexuality is presented, many young people have told us that the negative feelings created from such object lessons are so overwhelming that they struggle to internalize any other meaning from the lesson.

Latter-day Saints have also told us that when parents and leaders appeared uneasy or reluctant to teach them about sex, they began to feel apprehensive about the topic themselves. In fact many feel that parents and leaders like to use object lessons because it allows them to talk about sex—without taking about sex. If young people internalize these fretful emotions, such negative conditioning may have long-term consequences in later marriages when couples try to "re-program" their attitudes about modesty, sexuality, and intimacy.

Fear-based metaphors also tend to discourage an open dialogue between young people and their parents or leaders about sexuality. Often in this context, young people feel that if they ask questions or show any interest in the topic, they may be thought of as "bad" or "dirty." Thus we shouldn't be surprised when young people gravitate to friends, the media, or other outside sources to learn about sexual issues—sources that are often not in harmony with Gospel values. Their personal experiences learning about sexual matters then becomes mostly a secretive one, where they recall reading anatomy books, watching TV programs, or doing internet searches under a cloak of secrecy, embarrassment, and shame.

While fear-based metaphors tend to teach about out-of-bounds behaviors (i.e., "sex before marriage is wrong," "masturbation is sinful," "don't use pornography," etc.), they struggle to convey the doctrinal principles or reasons behind these restrictions. This often leaves young people unpersuaded as to why they should try to live a sexually pure life—and particularly in a world that is becoming more adept at getting them to be unchaste.

Many young people have also commented that fear-based metaphors made them feel that there was no way they could repent of or repair any sexual sins they may have already committed. The only message they often hear is the ideal of flaw-less sexual perfection, rather than one of sincere sexual progression. To young minds, images of burned dresses and wilted flower petals appear irreparable and permanent. Thus some are left to feel that they are the damaged goods that no one—including their Father in Heaven—will ever want.

Abstinence-Based Metaphors

While parents and leaders sometimes teach young people about sexuality using fear-based metaphors, our experience is that the more common object lessons fit into a group we call abstinence-based metaphors. These metaphors convey a "worth waiting for" message to young people, where sex is portrayed as a positive aspect of life when experienced within the context of marriage.

For some reason, many abstinence-based metaphors involve desirable food. For example, a counselor in the bishopric once brought freshly baked chocolate chip cookies to a combined youth lesson about chastity—on a Fast Sunday. As the aroma of the cookies spread throughout the room, he asked the youth if they would like to eat one. After they eagerly indicated they would love to have one of the cookies, the counselor then reminded the group that it was Fast Sunday. After their groans had subsided, the counselor then compared waiting to eat the cookies at the right time to waiting until marriage for sex.

Another young man told us about his deacon's quorum advisor who gave each young man two chocolate candies and told them, "If you bring these chocolates back next week, I'll give you ten chocolates." So the following week the boys who brought both their candies back were rewarded with the promised ten chocolates. Then the advisor said, "Now, for those who bring all ten chocolates back next week, I'll give you a whole bag of chocolates." You can see where the advisor was going with this. So at the end of the third week, the advisor used the example to teach the boys that delayed gratification brings bigger rewards and greater satisfactions compared to immediate gratification, and encouraged them to wait for the "bigger treat" that awaits them in marriage.

Now, some may be wondering what is so wrong with such abstinence-based metaphors? The flaw is rooted in what they fail to teach rather than in what they do teach; they are only partially correct because they are incomplete metaphors. Our interviews over the years have convinced us that such abstinence-based lessons may have at least three unintended negative side effects.

1) Chastity as Simply a Physical Issue

One of the primary pitfalls of abstinence-based lessons is that they unintentionally infer that chastity is simply a physical issue. The focus is on just sexual behaviors, and the timing of such behaviors. While behaviors are an important part of the law of chastity, they are not the heart of the law. Chastity and virtue are at the heart of the law, thus making it more of a spiritual issue that should first be embraced in our hearts and our minds before it is expressed in our behaviors. Unfortunately, abstinence-based object lessons tend to assume that all expressions of sexuality are similar in intent and purpose. And there is typically no acknowledgement that loving and lustful approaches to sexuality may occur before and after marriage. They incorrectly assume that all sexual expressions after marriage are inherently loving in nature—simply because they take place after a wedding. What is also not taught is that attitudes and motives of why spouses seek sexual union with each other can change, and thus become the true indicator of whether sexual behaviors are chaste or not. We may be chaste before and after we are married; we may also be unchaste before and after marriage. Simply put, the *whys* of sex in marriage matter more than the *whats* of sex.

2) Chastity as Simply an Individual Issue

Abstinence-based perspectives also tend to portray chastity as a character trait that one earns as a result of wise personal choices and worthiness. But a deeper appreciation of chastity is better understood in relationships between two people. Chastity is relational in nature because sex is designed to be an activity that involves others, and can thus convey either other-centered love or self-centered lust. When sex is compared to one person eating something such as food or candy, it implies that true sexual fulfillment comes from receiving, not from giving. Thus the sharing and other-centered aspects of sexuality are missing; and these are the key components that are vital in building a healthy and intimate marriage.

3) Chastity has a "Marriage Finish Line"

Perhaps the most troubling aspect of abstinence-based metaphors is that they convey the mistaken idea that the need for chastity ends at marriage; if young people can "just hold out" until they are married, they will not have to worry about chastity any more. Perhaps such reasoning motivates some couples to shorten their engagements and get married before they "make a mistake." But nothing could be further from the truth because there is no such thing as a "marriage finish line" with respect to chastity and personal purity. Chastity is one of the ongoing foundational principles of healthy and lasting marriages. Couples should be taught to keep their thoughts and actions chaste on their honeymoons and on into their marriages. So when understood correctly, marriage is not the end but a continuation of our quest for chastity and personal purity.

A New Metaphor

What, then, is the most fitting object lesson to use? you may ask. What would be the most appropriate metaphor to properly teach about sexuality? Our bold answer to the first question is that the best object lesson is no object lesson! Even if someone comes up with a clever object lesson that apparently gets past the pitfalls of fear-based and abstinence-based metaphors, using any object lesson still conveys that the instructor is uncomfortable with directly addressing the topic of sexuality. We are repeatedly told by young people that their great wish is to have their parents and leaders simply talk openly—and thoroughly—to them about sex. Regarding the second question, we think it is stated backwards; in other words, there is no adequate metaphor with which to compare sex because sex is the metaphor! So instead of asking *What parts of life may be compared to sex?* we should rather ask *How does sex help us better understand other parts of life?*—especially our discipleship and faithful progression as individuals and couples.

Questions to Ponder

1. *Which metaphor best describes how I learned about sex while growing up?*

2. *Do I feel fear or shame when I discuss sexuality?*

3. *Do I feel anxious or embarrassed when others talk about sex? If so, why?*

4. *Has fear, shame or other negative conditioning influenced my perceptions of sexuality? If so, how?*

5. *Does the principle of chastity change once a person is married?*

3

SEX AND SALVATION

The *Proclamation on the Family* states,

> *In the premortal realm, spirit sons and daughters knew and worshipped God as their Eternal Father and accepted His plan by which His children could obtain a physical body and gain earthly experience to progress toward perfection and ultimately realize their divine destiny as heirs of eternal life.*

Note how this prophetic statement ties together two key principles: obtaining a physical body—with all of its divinely-formed parts, passions, and sensations—and earthly experiences we need to progress toward perfection. This helps us appreciate that many of the important experiences we will have in this life will be connected to our bodies, and thus infused with sexuality.

A cycle begins in our younger years while growing up where we may struggle to make sense of intense sensual feelings and the power of the sexual response in our bodies. Later, in dating and courtship, we tend to pair up at least partially because of mutual sexual attractions. Then in marriage, much of our physical and emotional bonding is directly linked to sexuality; children are conceived through our sexual union. And at a young age our children begin the cycle anew as they become aware of their own sexual feelings. Now as parents, we want to appropriately guide our children as they walk on their own journey of sexual maturation. Indeed, much of our earthly lives involves sexual experience.

Sex is properly seen as a crucial and sacred aspect of salvation, and central to God's plan for the eternal destiny of His children. In fact it may be accurate to say that sexuality is about salvation, and salvation is about sexuality. How we express ourselves sexually is one of the most important tests of discipleship in determining couple and family unity, and whether we are on the path of righteous living. When the sexual part of our lives is aligned with our spiritual values and emotional and physical needs, this can help us build more unity and strength as couples as few other things can. On the other hand, when the sexual aspect of our marriage is out of alignment and not working well, we quickly become aware of how easily our relationships may erode, temptations may increase, and poor decisions may be made.

Each of us has been endowed with a powerful sexual nature that is beautiful and ordained of God.

> It was necessary that this power of creation have at least two dimensions: one, it must be strong; and two, it must be more or less constant. This power must be strong, for most men by nature seek adventure. Except for the compelling persuasion of these feelings, men would be reluctant to accept the responsibility of sustaining a home and a family. This power must be constant, too, for it becomes a binding tie in family life (Elder Boyd K. Packer, "Why Stay Morally Clean," *New Era*, July 1972, p.5). wtf?

Sex is not just a part of life we need to deal with while we focus on our real spiritual progression; sex is central to spiritual progression. One of the key tests of our mortal probation is whether we can learn to experience the wonders of our physical bodies in ways that build stronger relationships with God and with our spouse. Yet the Adversary is real, and he constantly entices us to express our sexual urges in ways that destroy rather than build. Because these strong physical yearnings are key to happy family life, it is vital that we find appropriate ways to experience these pleasurable aspects of our bodies, to where we are strengthening our marriages and our families. Sex, then, may be one of the most apt metaphors to gauge our spiritual well being and our trajectory on the pathway to salvation.

Sexual Fragmentation

Unfortunately, rather than integrating sexuality and discipleship, our culture is moving toward what we call sexual fragmentation. Sexual fragmentation occurs whenever the spiritual, physical, and emotional components of human sexuality are separated or devalued. Speaking on the topic of sexuality, Elder Jeffrey R. Holland taught that one of the most important truths of this dispensation is that "the spirit and the body are the soul of man (D&C 88:15), and that when they are separated we "cannot receive a fullness of joy" (D&C 93:34; see also Jeffrey R. Holland, "Of Souls, Symbols, and Sacraments," BYU devotional address, 1988). This means that to experience a fullness of joy in our marriages and in our lives, we need to understand how to integrate—not separate—the spiritual and physical aspects of sexuality within the total relationship we share as husbands and wives.

Spirit-Only Fragmentation

We are aware of two primary types of sexual fragmentation that are common among Church members: the first we call spirit-only fragmentation, and the second we call body-only fragmentation. Spirit-only fragmentation prioritizes the spirit over the body, and views sexual desire as a mortal—or moral—weakness to overcome in the quest for spiritual progression. This perspective is one of sex *or* salvation, rather than sex *and* salvation. In this context, devoted love is characterized as inherently spiritual, good, and affiliated with God, while sexual passions are viewed as inherently carnal, evil, and affiliated with the Adversary.

In her writing on this subject, Laura Brotherson, an LDS sex educator, has labeled this type of negative perspective toward sex as "Good Girl Syndrome." She has identified a common pattern for many young women in the Church who believe that "good girls" shouldn't have sexual feelings or desires. Although both men and women can have this type of sex conditioning or thinking, it has been found to be more common in women. Signs of Good Girl Syndrome include negative feelings about sex and one's body; discomfort or embarrassment in discussing sexual matters; an underlying belief that sex is wrong, dirty, or sinful; the development of inappropriate inhibitions; and guilt, shame, or awkwardness associated with sexual relations (Brotherson, *And They Were Not Ashamed*, pp. 1-4).

An example of this type of fragmentation is found in the questions asked by Alex that we shared in Chapter One. You may recall that Alex sent a note to his professor expressing concerns about his wife's "improper attitudes" about sex, including her desire to experience the fullness of her sexual response. He fears that her comfort with sex means that she is not "spiritually in tune," and that her desires are not normal. Alex is concerned that his wife may not be a "good girl."

Views such as those expressed by Alex are often based on a distorted view of the "natural man" principle discussed in Mosiah 3:19. In this verse of scripture we are taught that "the natural man is an enemy to God," and that becoming a true saint only occurs as someone "yields to the enticing of the Holy Spirit, and putteth off the natural man and becometh a saint through the atonement of Christ the Lord." Some Latter-day Saints view the term "natural" in this verse as a reference to our physical bodies, and that spiritual progression occurs as we focus our lives only on spiritual sensations rather than the so-called carnal sensations associated with our bodies. However, such a perspective is not in harmony with the restored doctrine of the "soul," and the "fullness of joy" (see D&C 93:34) that the scriptures teach can only be experienced when the spirit and body are united eternally.

Thus when it comes to marriage preparation, spirit-only fragmentation conveys the message that purity—typically defined as abstaining from sex—is the only needed preparation for sexuality in marriage. Such fragmentation mistakenly promises that satisfying sex is either an inevitable outcome of love, or that sexual satisfaction is something with which spiritually-minded couples should not be concerned.

One of our primary motivations for writing this book is our belief that fear-based and abstinence-based metaphors are prevalent in the current sexual culture among Latter-day Saints, and feed this spirit-only fragmentation. That, combined with the reluctance of parents and others to address these matters frankly and consistently, leaves many Latter-day Saints struggling with feelings that sex is wrong, dirty, and shameful, and contrary to a spiritual way of life. This type of sexual fragmentation may foster many negative consequences in our quest for healthy sexuality and marital intimacy.

The Divine Purposes of Sexuality

Overcoming spirit-only fragmentation requires that we develop an abiding testimony of the origins of sexual desire and the divine purposes of sex. President Spencer W. Kimball once quoted the popular evangelist, Reverend Billy Graham, stating:

> *The Bible celebrates sex and its proper use, presenting it as God-created, God-ordained, God-blessed. It makes plain that God himself implanted the physical magnetism between the sexes for two reasons: for the propagation of the human race, and for the expression of that kind of love between man and wife that makes for true oneness. His commandment*

*to the first man and woman to be "one flesh" was as important as his
command to "be fruitful and multiply (Ensign, May 1974, pp. 7–8).*

Thus, the first divine purpose for sexuality in God's plan is for couples to participate in the creation of physical bodies (procreation) for His spirit children. This
ongoing process of creation is one of the central doctrines of God's plan for our
salvation. Marriage is the divinely decreed institution, and sexual union of spouses
is the divinely decreed process to bring about such procreation.

The second and more common divine purpose for the expression of sexual intimacy is to unify spouses—with each other and with God. Prophets have taught
that sexual intimacy in marriage is for spouses to express love for one another, to
bond with one another, and to experience pleasure and joy.

> *Our natural affections are planted in us by the Spirit of God for a wise
> purpose, and they are the very main-springs of life and happiness; they
> are the cement of all virtuous and heavenly society; they are the essence
> of charity, or love.... There is not a more pure and holy principle in
> existence than the affection which glows in the bosom of a virtuous man
> for his companion.... The fact is, God made man, male and female,
> [and] he planted in their bosoms those affections which are calculated
> to promote their happiness and union (Parker Pratt Robison, ed.,
> Writings of Parley Parker Pratt, Salt Lake City: Deseret News Press,
> 1952, pp. 52–53).*

President Spencer W. Kimball also taught:

> *Sex is for procreation and expression of love. It is the destiny of men and
> women to join together to make eternal family units. In the context of
> lawful marriage, the intimacy of sexual relations is right and divinely
> approved. There is nothing unholy or degrading about sexuality in itself,
> for by that means men and women join in a process of creation and in
> an expression of love (President Spencer W. Kimball, Teachings, 312).*

Our prophetic leaders have consistently taught that sexual intimacy is a good
and righteous part of married life. President Spencer W. Kimball also taught that
"husband and wife are authorized; in fact, they are commanded to have proper
sex when they are married for time and eternity" (*President Spencer W. Kimball,*

Teachings, 312). President Ezra Taft Benson emphasized that "sex was created and established by our Heavenly Father for sacred, holy, and high purposes" (*President Ezra Taft Benson, Teachings*, 409).

Repentance from Sexual Sin

We have found that spirit-only fragmentation is particularly common among individuals and couples who have known sexual transgression. Experiences with pornography and premarital sexual transgressions often result in feelings of shame, deep regret, and low self-worth, which are then woven into their overall views of sexuality. These negative perspectives can become deep rooted if parents and leaders are reluctant to frankly teach about repentance from sexual transgression. They may fear that young people may take more liberties if they believe it is easy to repent of sexual transgressions, or think that sexual sin is not a big deal. Parents and leaders should overcome such reluctance, because if young people hold an improper understanding of 1) the seriousness of sexual transgression as well as 2) the cleansing power of Christ's atonement, it may contribute to lasting spirit-only fragmentation, and eventually manifest itself in dating and marriage relationships.

Many years ago an object lesson was used by some church members to teach about the consequences of sin and the nature of repentance. This object lesson involved hammering nails into a board and telling the class "this is like sinning." Then the teacher would remove the nails and tell the class "this is like repenting." The moral of the lesson, however, was when the teacher would hold up the board and say "but the holes are still there!" While well meaning, this teacher had an uninformed view of repentance and the atonement of Jesus Christ. As a result, many members of the church have become discouraged and hurt by such distorted portrayals.

In stark contrast, the Savior himself has told us that "though your sins be as scarlet, they shall be as white as snow; though they be red like crimson, they shall be as wool." (Isaiah 1:5) The correct doctrine explains that the Lord does not just remove the nails from our board, nor does he just cover up the holes so that no one will notice; He gives us a whole new board. When we sincerely repent, the atonement of Jesus Christ has power to cleanse us, restore us, and strengthen us to withstand future temptations. This is true for all of our sins—including sexual transgressions.

Body-Only Fragmentation

While spirit-only fragmentation is common among Latter-day Saints and other under-sexually educated, religiously conservative people, body-only fragmentation is most common in modern society at large. Body-only fragmentation occurs when the physical sensations of sexual response are disconnected from spiritual meanings, emotional bonding, and relationship patterns. The central tenet of body-only fragmentation is that true sexual fulfillment in our individual lives and in our marriages is only found by discovering ways to stimulate our bodies so that we can experience desired levels of sexual arousal and sensation.

In its most base form, body-only fragmentation completely separates sex from relationships. Young adults today are all too familiar with terms such as *hook-ups*, *NCMO*, and *friends with benefits*—phrases describing two people sharing various forms of physical contact outside of the so-called constraints of committed relationships.

Unfortunately, body-only fragmentation has also become a common view with which many couples approach their marital sexuality. Spouses may begin to believe that sexuality is the same as intimacy, and that because they have sex—they are intimate. Such faulty thinking fuels the myth that sex is inherently intimate; and it reinforces the notion that physical responses—such as arousal and orgasm—are sufficient indicators of intimacy. Warning us how intimacy is not sexuality, Elder Jeffrey R. Holland taught:

> *Fragmentation enables its users to counterfeit intimacy.... If we relate to each other in fragments, at best we miss full relationships. At worst, we manipulate and exploit others for our gratification. Sexual fragmentation can be particularly harmful because it gives powerful physiological rewards which, though illusionary, can temporarily persuade us to overlook the serious deficits in the overall relationship.... Sexual fragmentation is particularly harmful because it is particularly deceptive. The intense human intimacy that should be enjoyed and symbolized by sexual union is counterfeited by sensual episodes which suggest—but cannot deliver—acceptance, understanding, and love. Such encounters mistake the end for the means....* ("Of Souls, Symbols, and Sacraments," Jeffrey R. Holland, BYU Devotional, 12 Jan 1988).

Consider Jenny and Steve's sexual relationship which we introduced in Chapter One. You may remember Jenny was concerned about her declining interest in sex, and Steve was suggesting that they get a sexual technique book and try to spice things up with some variety in their lovemaking. Unable to discuss their differences openly, Jenny was beginning to fake arousal during sex in order to finish sooner. Jenny and Steve's relationship is an example of body-only fragmentation in a number of ways. Steve seems to be equating his wife's growing dissatisfaction with sex as an indicator that she is unhappy with the technique of how they have sex, while Jenny's greatest concerns are about the emotional depth of their overall relationship. She wants Steve to be interested in her as a whole person— not just attracted to her body. For her, the problem is not the sex as much as it is the symbols. But her pretending to enjoy sex rather than share her real feelings with her husband is hurting both spouses, to where they feel emotionally distant from each other. This is a common consequence when body-only fragmentation is present in a relationship.

Professional Endorsement of Body-Only Fragmentation

In fairness to Steve and Jenny, they are not unique, nor did they invent body-only fragmentation. In fact, Steve and others spouses who have fallen into this way of thinking are simply following the dominant sexual script in our society. The prevalence of body-only fragmentation in modern culture stems in part from the "naturalization of sex" that began in the 1960s and 1970s among so-called sex therapists, couple counselors, and marriage educators. This "naturalized" approach to sex is typified by the "sexual response cycle" introduced by Masters and Johnson, which produced a focus on orgasm as both a finish line of sex and as the primary criteria of "good sex." Modern healthcare providers and social scientists have adopted a medical model of sexuality that focuses on physical functioning (i.e. body-only), and labels sexual function or dysfunction according to physical markers of sexual arousal (e.g., arousal disorders, orgasm disorders, etc.). There is very little discussion of personal growth, sexual meaning, and emotional intimacy between spouses.

Going with the flow of these trends, sexual health professionals for the last 30 to 40 years have focused on the physiology, chemistry, and neurology of sexual response, and have stirred a public obsession over the mechanics of sex. The result has been the emergence of "modern sex therapy," complete with advice manuals and slick websites that confuse physical reactions with intimate experience, and purposefully ignore sexual motivations and meaning. Ironically, modern sex therapy is currently experiencing a paradigmatic crisis as issues related to decreased sexual desire are now the number one presenting problem of couples seeking help. This highlights the fact that our society's obsession with physical functioning is not resulting in fulfilling sexual relationships or lasting marriages. Yet this should not surprise us, because such body-only fragmentation misses the truth that in order to achieve genuine sexual satisfaction, it is the emotional and relationship aspects of sexuality that will always be the most salient.

Questions to Ponder

1. *Some people believe that really enjoying sex is inappropriate, because sex is dirty or evil. Others don't associate sex with spirituality, emotions or a relationship. How has my sexual development been influenced by these sexually fragmented ideas?*

2. *How might I be "counterfeiting intimacy" in my relationship? Do I substitute other things—including sex—for true intimacy?*

3. *Mark the figure below to represent where your relationship may be on the three dimensions of sexuality. If you are not in the ideal, how might you modify your relationship?*

Three Dimensions of Sexuality

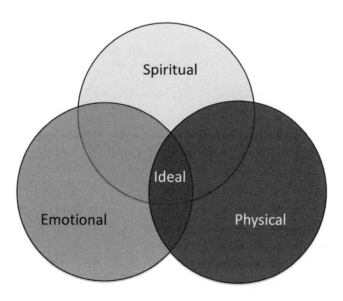

SECTION II

A MODEL OF SEXUAL WHOLENESS

4

A MODEL OF SEXUAL WHOLENESS

Avoiding sexual fragmentation and developing sexual wholeness in marriage is a life-long process, and must be grounded in correct understandings of intimacy and sexuality. While many of the questions we are asked as professors by individuals and couples focus on specific aspects of sex, such questions typically reflect either an insufficient understanding or an incorrect understanding of the main principles of sexuality. Additionally, sexuality is always intertwined with personal maturity and the idea of growth. Yet sexual wholeness takes more than simply learning principles or facts; it requires an ongoing commitment to the quality of our marriages, and courage to openly explore feelings, motives, behaviors, and experiences related to our sexual relationship.

Healthy sexuality and fulfilling intimacy is founded upon two primary aspects of marriage relationships. First, spouses must understand how to create true intimacy in their marriage. True intimacy can be experienced only when spouses interact with each other in ways that meet each other's personal needs. So when we address sexual questions, we always encourage couples to *focus on meeting true needs*—this is a key to fostering sexual wholeness. We can never get enough of what we don't really need; but when true needs are satisfied—it is enough. Talking about the nature and dynamics of couple intimacy can help spouses understand how their sexual relationship may be influencing their overall relationship, and likewise how other aspects of their relationship may be influencing their sexual experiences.

For the second key aspect, spouses must appreciate all facets of human *sexual nature,* and try to avoid any form of sexual fragmentation in their marriage relationship. Our divinely-created souls consist of a spirit body and a physical body, each with its unique capacities and needs. This is our true nature. Our spirit bodies endow us with the potential to love, a desire for meaning, and an innate need to be emotionally connected to other people. This spiritual self is also comprised of spiritual senses, emotional feelings, and a need for belonging in lasting relationships. Our physical bodies endow us with the capacity for enjoyment, pleasure, and contentment. This physical part of our nature consists of our physical needs as well as capacity for stimulating experience.

Looking through these two "lenses" of the doctrine of the soul provides insight into all of human experience, but it gives special insight into understanding human sexuality and marital intimacy. In particular, it teaches us that sexual health and happiness comes when we express our sexuality in ways that satisfy true needs of both dimensions—for our spouse and ourselves.

Spouses' Needs and Creating Intimacy

Having our needs fulfilled is indeed the key to creating true intimacy. Even though this concept is simple enough it requires, then, that spouses understand both their own and their spouse's needs. While most of us may be keenly aware of our need for food, sleep, and shelter, we may not be as aware of other needs—both emotional and physical—particularly those that are expressed and met within sexual union. And spouses often struggle to understand their own needs, let alone the needs of their mate.

Unfortunately, most books and websites about sex don't help much when it comes to understanding true humans needs. Often these sources make the problem worse by ignoring emotional needs altogether. The sad truth is that most books about sex are exactly that—books just about sex. They focus on the physical act of sex by emphasizing techniques and positions, as if sex were just another physical activity that spouses do with each other. Nevertheless, as divinely created beings with both spirits and bodies, all people have a fundamental need for intimacy; this intimacy is divided into two primary heads: the *need to **belong***, and the *need to **become***. The need to belong includes our innate desire to be loved by and connected to others; the need to become includes our divine drive to develop our full potential. While these two needs may be expressed in a variety of ways, they are still central to our sense of sexual wholeness.

Linking sex to our need to belong and to become helps us see that sex is not a frivolous thing a couple does, it is a core part of their relationship. Our need to belong and to become make us *meaning-making* creatures. We create meanings or symbols from the experiences in our lives, and sexual experiences may be some of the most symbolic. Elder Jeffrey R. Holland has also taught that a sexual union between a man and a woman is intended to be a special and transformative symbol of their relationship:

> *Human intimacy, that sacred, physical union ordained of God for a married couple, deals with a symbol that demands special sanctity. Such an act of love between a man and a woman is—or certainly was ordained to be—a symbol of their total union: union of their hearts, their hopes, their lives, their love, their family, their future, their every-thing* ("Of Souls, Symbols, and Sacraments," Jeffrey R. Holland, BYU Devotional, 12 Jan 1988).

When a husband takes time to listen intently to his wife, it symbolizes that she is an interesting person and a priority to her husband. But if he is often inattentive or non-disclosing during their conversations, she may feel disconnected and devalued. Likewise, when a wife initiates sex with her husband, it symbolizes that he is desirable and attractive. But if a pattern develops where a wife rarely initiates sex, he may feel vulnerable and become hesitant in expressing his own sexual desires. Additionally, when a husband disciplines his own arousal during sex to allow his wife to become equally aroused, he communicates without words that he wants this to be a shared experience rather than a selfish one.

It is impossible for humans to engage in meaningless sex because sex always creates and conveys meanings. These meanings will reveal how much spouses' needs are being met, as well as the depth of true intimacy in their relationship. So when spouses focus on meeting each other's needs—for belonging and for becoming—they may come to appreciate that sex is a highly symbolic part of their relationship that communicates the depth of love and concern they have for each other. This should encourage them to be responsive to each other, and seek out mutually enjoyable experiences that can build their relationship.

The Three Dimensions of Human Sexual Nature

As we noted earlier, one of the vital truths of the restored Gospel is that "the spirit and the body are the soul of man" (D&C 88:15), and that when the spirit and body are separated, men and women "cannot receive a fullness of joy" (D&C 93:34). In this simple truth, we discover a key to avoid the trap of sexual fragmentation, and the foundation for developing sexual wholeness as individuals and as couples. This doctrine of the soul teaches us that all sexual experiences as mortals affect both our bodies and our spirits. It also teaches us that our spirits are the source of our emotions, feelings, and thought, and that in order to have sexual

Figure 4.1 – Dimensions of Sexual Nature

fulfillment we need to appreciate how they are enmeshed with the physical reactions of our bodies, and vice versa (see Figure 4.1).

The Spiritual Dimension

Because we are spiritual beings—having a mortal experience, it is in our nature to seek meaning and purpose in our lives. The *Proclamation on the Family* teaches that each of us "is a beloved spirit son or daughter of heavenly parents, and, as such, each has a divine nature and destiny." Thus we all have an innate desire to progress in the noble aspects of our lives. So when we live according to God's will and have faith in His divine plan for us, we feel contentment and peace because we are filling "the measure of our creation" (D&C 88:5). But when we feel a lack of progression in our lives, that same divine nature gives us feelings in our hearts or ideas in our minds that something is amiss, leaving us to feel restless or frustrated. When such lack of progression is tied to sin and being out of alignment with God's commandments, we often feel a sense of unworthiness and shame, and see a decrease in our faith.

This innate desire to progress is also a part of our sexual nature, where we all seek for *sexual meaning*. Thus when our sexual expressions are in alignment with God's purposes, we sense that sex has meaning and purpose in our lives; it becomes inseparably linked to strong feelings of love for our spouse and for God. This quietly endows us with a sense of worthiness, and a growing appreciation for the positive role sex was designed to play in our lives. At times, however, individuals or couples may express their sexuality in shallow or meaningless ways that are not in alignment with God's divine purposes for sex. When this happens, our spiritual nature reacts and causes us to feel less content and unfulfilled.

The Physical Dimension

The current discussion about human sexuality in both popular and professional circles is dominated by the size of body parts, sexual techniques, and products that claim to enhance our physical responses. Even sexual desire is seen as emerging from physical origins, as reflected in popular notions of "libido," "sex drive," or "horniness." This has its professional origins in Freud's psychoanalytic theory that viewed humans as having an involuntary, physically-generated sexual energy that must be expressed. The notion of human's having an involuntary physical sex drive is often used to rationalize inappropriate sexual expression—whether before or during marriage. Such physical-only perspectives fail to include the spiritual and emotional dimensions of our sexual nature, which emphasize the voluntary and controllable capacity for sexual expression. True expressions of love and commitment were never intended to be just one dimensional manifestations of genes and hormones.

Even though spiritual perspectives caution us to not embrace lustful perspectives and practices that may lead to body-only fragmentation, we should not discount the significance of the physical dimension of our sexual nature. Again, the doctrine of the soul teaches us that our physical bodies are essential to our happiness—both in this life and in the world to come. In fact, one of the major purposes of this life is for the spirit children of God to receive physical bodies, and that after this life and through the power of the resurrection we can live like our Heavenly Parents—with an immortal *physical* body. Thus living a virtuous life—now or then—does not require us to reject the joy of our physical senses, rather it enlarges our capacity for a full and satisfying enjoyment of them.

We each have an innate desire for *sexual satisfaction*. The bodies of both men and women are endowed with divinely created "arousal systems" that are linked to the natural processes of attraction, attachment, and touch. Because of the physical portion of our nature, we innately desire and respond to physical closeness and touch in ways that can provide deep feelings of pleasure and satisfaction. The fullest expression of this need is when husbands and wives become "one flesh" (Genesis 2:4), thus uniting both their spirit bodies and their physical bodies.

The Emotional Dimension

Each of us has a fundamental need to be deeply connected to others; this is a core part of our spiritual nature and is shared by all people on earth. Elder Bruce C. Hafen explains, "People simply desire to be connected with others, especially in close relationships. They are feeling the longing to belong.… Both our theology and the feelings of our hearts make us want to belong, now and eternally, to the father of our Spirits, to his Son, and to those we love on earth" (Elder Bruce C. Hafen, *The Belonging Heart*, pp. 9-11). Through the fulfillment of this need we discover genuine security and happiness, as well as lasting motivation to trust, love, and sacrifice for others. Through such belonging and unselfish investment in others, we develop a more complete sense of happiness and well-being.

Our innate need for emotional attachment is another part of our sexual nature, and includes *sexual belonging*. When sexual intimacy fosters a sense of understanding and appreciation between spouses, it then reduces anxiety and increases emotional security within the relationship. This can become a virtuous reinforcing cycle as emotional security fosters satisfying sexual intimacy, and satisfying sexual intimacy can in turn build emotional security. Nevertheless, the opposite may also occur as emotional insecurity leads to struggles with sexual intimacy, and problems with sexual intimacy can in turn aggravate fragile feelings of insecurity. These patterns—for better or worse—help us appreciate the critical roles that commitment, attachment, and strict loyalty play in sexual wholeness in marriage.

Emotional security in couple relationships is founded upon courage, vulnerability, and a willingness to trust your spouse. Without emotional security, the natural vulnerability of such close relationships can become threatening; thus a fear of rejection may constrain how people behave in intimate situations. And when this happens, there is less authenticity, disclosure, and mutual reliance. Interestingly—yet fairly, vulnerability is a gateway to both true intimacy and cruel pain; we may choose to minimize the risk of pain in marriage by not being vulnerable, but in so doing we also reduce our capacity to experience true intimacy. This is why emotional security is such a key part of the personal maturity we should strive to develop, thus enabling us to form and maintain a loving and lasting marriage relationship.

In contrast with the physical dimension of our sexual nature which gives us innate cravings to experience sexual satisfaction ourselves, the emotional dimension of our sexual nature provides us with the surprising yet welcome capacity to experience profound fulfillment in the sexual satisfaction we may provide for our spouse. Our emotional nature makes us relational beings—interconnected; in addition to our need to belong and to become is our need to express true concern for the wellbeing of others, or what we term charity. It is to this part of our natures that Christ was referring when He taught, "he that findeth his life shall lose it, and whosoever will lose his life for my sake shall find it." (Matt 16:25) By divine law, true happiness cannot be found in simply seeking to satisfy our own desires and needs; it must include meeting the needs of others, and fulfilling their need to be loved. In marriage then, this is an opportunity for us to help our spouses meet their wants and needs.

Questions to ponder
1. *How do I allow myself to be known?*
2. *What hampers (or encourages) me to divulge my feelings?*
3. *Do I always need to be seen in a positive light, or can I expose feelings that may be uncomfortable, negative or sensitive?*

4. *How do I respond when my spouse exposes his/her feelings that challenge how I think or how I behave?*

5. *If living a virtuous life does not require us to reject the joy that may come from our physical senses, but instead enables a deeper and more satisfying enjoyment of them, am I participating in such a life?*

6. *How do I help meet my spouse's need to be loved?*

5

True Intimacy: Belonging and Becoming

In these next two chapters we discuss in more detail the emotional needs of *belonging* and *becoming*. This is a lifelong process that couples need to commit to in order to meet their needs in marriage. Our purpose is to highlight the end goal of our model of sexual wholeness; by first understanding the desired *destination*, couples may appreciate and more readily embrace additional parts of the *journey* we discuss in subsequent chapters. Following our more in depth treatment of the nature of intimacy in these next two chapters, we will then re-visit the three dimensions of our sexual natures, and discuss in detail how fostering the specific desires associated with these dimensions promotes lasting intimacy in marriage.

Belonging and *Becoming*

The Need for Belonging

In the scriptural account of the Creation, God declared: "It [is] not good that man should be alone" (Moses 3:18). In this statement, our Father in Heaven acknowledges a fundamental part of our divine nature: a need for love and belonging in enduring relationships. In particular this scripture infers our need for romantic belonging in an enduring pair-bond with an eternal spouse. Thus God instituted marriage and directed that a man shall "leave his father and his mother, and shall cleave unto his wife; and they shall be one flesh" (Moses 3:24). Commenting on this "longing for belonging," Elder Bruce C. Hafen and his wife, Marie K. Hafen, noted:

> *We all carry deep inside ourselves an inborn longing to belong that naturally draws us to certain people, beginning with our mother and father, then extending to others as we grow older, including our spouses, our children, and ultimately our Father in Heaven. The fulfillment of this longing leads to the achievement of humankind's deepest aspirations* (Bruce C. Hafen and Marie K. Hafen, *The Belonging Heart,* pp. x-xi).

This longing to belong is shared by all people. Although our society tends to champion independence and not relying upon others, this does not change our fundamental need to be deeply connected to others. In fact, by overemphasizing the value of independence, we may miss the need for interdependence and belonging. By celebrating independence, we may be wary of becoming too "needy" or "dependent" in close relationships. In fact, when we ask our students if they would like to marry a "needy person," no one answers affirmatively. They are typically surprised when we tell them that they may have a difficult time finding a spouse then, since all of us are needy; we all have needs that we cannot fulfill on our own. We strengthen our emotional security when we learn to trust, rely upon, and confide in others—rather than believing we can always take care of ourselves.

While writing books on the topic of "longing for belonging," Elder and Sister Hafen were introduced to the Japanese concept of *amae,* a word for which no English equivalent exists. The Hafens note that amae "describes the innate need and desire within each person to depend on and feel connected to other people, especially in relationships of love and intimacy. In a sense, [this] is the desire to receive love. Through the fulfillment of our amae we find not only security, but also freedom and meaning" (Bruce C. Hafen and Marie Hafen, *The Belonging Heart,* p.21).

Notice how *amae* is best described as the "desire to receive love." In gospel terms, charity includes the *giving* of Christ-like love, and *amae* is the *receiving* of Christ-like love. Maybe this is why charity is the greatest gift of the Spirit (1 Corinthians 13:13), because it allows us to fulfill the deepest and most basic of others' needs—to be loved and cared for. Additionally, the principle of *amae* gives us insights into the power and promise of the Atonement of Jesus Christ. As Elder Hafen explains, "The gospel's most fundamental promise is the *At-one-ment* of Jesus Christ, which offers the assurance of returning us to unity with God in eternal satisfaction of our *amae*" (p. 25). Thus, the atonement not only has power to make us one with God, but also one with our spouses in marriage—fulfilling our most profound longing to love and to be loved in eternal relationships.

The Need for Becoming

While it is part of our nature to desire closeness in permanent relationships, ironically we cannot escape the truth that we are each unique individuals as well. The *Encyclopedia of Mormonism* states:

> *There is no more stirring truth in God's revealed word than the idea that each individual personality is unique, eternal, independent, and possesses free agency. And it is the gospel's purpose to develop that personality to its utmost potential, as expressed in the doctrine of eternal progression, which can lead to ever-increasing meaning and freedom for each living soul* (Encyclopedia of Mormonism, 1992, p. 692).

Thus on the one hand, while each of us is a relational being who desires belonging in permanent relationships, and on the other hand we are independent souls who need to develop and express our personal potential. In short, we have an innate need—a drive—to become all that we possibly can become.

One of the more profound doctrines of the restored gospel is that each of us has always existed in some essential form, and that each of us will continue to exist forever. We read in the book of Abraham that the "intelligences that were organized before the world was" created "have no beginning; they existed before, they shall have no end, they shall exist after, for they are...eternal" (Abraham 3:18, 20). And the Lord revealed in modern times that "man was also in the beginning with God. Intelligence, or light of truth, was not created or made, neither indeed can be" (D&C 93:29).

We each feel a need to develop to our fullest potential, to become what our unique combination of attributes and talents intended us to become. This behooves each of us to live authentically, to be true to who we are and how we should experience the world. One of the important aspects of growing up and entering adulthood is appropriately expressing our personal passions and identity.

Recognizing and then fostering this need for becoming is also part of creating intimacy in marriage. In fact, an excellent way to determine whether a marriage relationship is healthy or unhealthy is to find out how much the becoming needs of each spouse are either fostered and encouraged—or diminished and constrained. President Gordon B. Hinckley said:

> *Respect [for one's spouse] comes of recognition that each of us is a son or daughter of God, endowed with something of His divine nature, that each is an individual entitled to expression and cultivation of individual talents and deserving of forbearance, of patience, of understanding, of courtesy, of thoughtful consideration. True love is not so much a matter of romance as it is a matter of anxious concern for the wellbeing of one's companion* (Ensign, *June 1971, p. 71).*

Intimacy: Bringing Together *Belonging* and *Becoming*

On the surface it may appear that our need for belonging and our need for becoming are somewhat at odds with each other in marriage; Will our need for individual becoming inevitably be constrained by the bonds of belonging? Will true unity between spouses be undermined by our unique needs? Gladly, it is not an either/or proposition; true intimacy in marriage is found at the *intersection* of belonging and becoming. In fact, when spouses strive to balance these two types of needs, they will begin to see the fullness of intimacy that is available in their marriage. This is true of their sexual relationship as well as their overall relationship. The practical place to begin is to engage in a pattern of interaction that fosters *authentic belonging.* Authentic belonging occurs when spouses feel loved and cherished—without reservation—for who they truly are. Being known and still loved. When we know and are known—and still are accepted, spouses can then feel that both their need to belong and their need to become are being simultaneously met.

The origin of the word *intimacy* is found in the Latin term *intimus* which simply means "inner" or "inmost." Thus, an *intimate relationship* is one in which two people share with each other their inner selves. This involves the disclosure of personal feelings, thoughts, desires, and experiences. Notice how this describes a *process* or a way of interacting within a relationship. In modern usage, however, we typically use the term *intimacy* to convey an *outcome* rather than a process, and specifically only a positive outcome associated with feelings of agreement, compatibility, and validation. Surprisingly, the term *intimate experience* is rarely used to describe an uncomfortable or unsupportive exchange with one's spouse, even though such may be the most revealing of spouses' inmost thoughts and feelings.

This shift in how we use the word *intimacy* is significant because it reflects how many of us have come to regard intimacy in marriage. Many believe that intimacy only involves positive interactions and positive feelings; that intimacy should always feel good. The problem with this way of thinking is that when deeply personal disagreements or differences are shared between spouses, it may then be taken as a threat to marital closeness and well-being. Perhaps this is why in our earlier example Jenny won't tell Steve about her concerns, or why Shannon's husband refuses to talk about his patterns of media use.

Thus we should now see that the process of true intimacy requires spouses to share their whole inner-selves with each other, which in the natural course of life, may include the parts of agreement and similarity as well as the parts of disagreement and difference. At its core, intimacy is a process of knowing and being known. Curiously, one of the terms used in the Bible to denote sexual intercourse was to *know* each other, such as "And Adam *knew* Eve his wife" (Genesis 4:1). But as we have explained, there may be additional meaning to that scripture. Thus true intimacy that creates genuine closeness is a process that involves authentic disclosure and sharing between spouses. Sometimes this process may be energizing or validating, and other times it may leave spouses feeling wilted or vulnerable.

Couples who complain about a "lack of intimacy" in their marriage may assume it is because they don't see enough similarity or agreement between spouses. But such an approach to couple relationships mistakes the ends for the means; it suggests that couples should try to be intimate (the ends) *in spite of* their differences (the wrong means), rather than recognizing that husbands and wives can only be truly intimate (the ends) *in* their differences (the right means).

We refer to these two very different aspects of intimacy as the *Intimacy of Validation* and the *Intimacy of Confrontation*. The intimacy of validation fosters the need for belonging; the intimacy of confrontation fosters the need for becoming. Both aspects should be founded upon charity for one's spouse, trust in each other, and a sincere desire to strengthen the marriage relationship. Spouses show true charity for one another by giving each other a sense of value, acceptance and belonging. And as we have learned, charity also prompts us to be deeply committed to both our own and our partner's growth. Thus, the intimacy of validation involves loving someone *just the way they are;* there is no hint of a hidden agenda to try to change the other person against their will. This process includes the sharing of similarities and consensus, where spouses build feelings of trust, closeness, affection, and mutual support.

However, spouses must also develop the maturity to engage in the process of sharing differences and conflict as part of the intimacy of confrontation. This includes loving someone *for who they can be,* and being committed to helping the marriage relationship reach its fullest potential. When we are truly committed to such progression, we should feel dissatisfied with important aspects of our lives that may need to change. Then the next step is for spouses to be willing to confront weakness, immaturity, and differences—whether in themselves or their spouses. In this process of intimacy, spouses may feel vulnerable, hurt, fearful, angry, and unappreciated. As such, it will require courage, sensitivity, authenticity, and a willingness to find deeper understanding through conflict.

Questions to Ponder

1. *Do I have a healthy balance of belonging and becoming? Does my spouse?*

2. *Does unity undermine uniqueness?*

3. *In what ways can a focus on becoming help me develop intimacy in my relationship?*

4. *How do I handle the intimacy of validation and the intimacy of confrontation? Is one type of intimacy more difficult for me? Why?*

5. *Do I encourage independent thought and independent behavior in my relationship?*

6. *Do I authentically disclose, or do I tend to withhold some information?*

7. *Do I give genuine acknowledgment or do I tend to dismiss the feelings and ideas of my spouse?*

6

THE RESURRECTION OF EROTICISM

We have found that most relationship advice given to couples by both professional and personal sources emphasizes just the need for togetherness and belonging. And so most spouses know that they need to support, validate, and connect with one another—even though some may struggle trying. These aspects of the intimacy of validation fit within the typical "relationship script" that most spouses have for what makes a good marriage.

However, we have also found that the *need for becoming* and the importance of ongoing personal growth are underappreciated aspects of marriage relationships , and thus not usually included in marriage advice talks—especially as it relates to the quality of couples' sexual relationships. Therefore, many couples come to marriage not fully appreciating how the personal growth of each spouse is an essential catalyst for creating and maintaining a spark of vitality in their sexual relationship; this spark can infuse their whole relationship with a sense of creativity, energy, and excitement. So if belonging is not properly balanced with a measure of becoming, marital sexuality runs a higher risk of turning mundane and predictable—which may then dampen the vitality of their whole relationship. To avoid such a decline, some couples may need to re-prioritize their time and re-discover the erotic part of their marriage; in cases where there was fear-based sexual conditioning, a couple may need to discover eroticism for the first time.

There are many types of personal becoming, and each involves developing your talents, reaching your potential, and experiencing a broad range of life. Examples include spiritual progression, where each of us can develop deeper faith in the

Savior, increase our spiritual gifts, and develop fuller devotion to living the gospel and serving others; intellectual growth, where learning expands our mental capacity that we can apply in beneficial ways; talent development, which is a type of becoming that involves self-discovery, and brings deep personal satisfaction as we share our personal gifts with others. All of such types of becoming are important parts of living an abundant and authentic life. Another important type of personal becoming is *sexual becoming*—the process of discovering our sexual capacity, and learning to authentically and appropriately express our personal sexual desires. This process culminates in a *shared* becoming process where spouses may experience the full sexual potential of their bodies in ways that strengthen their relationship.

Eroticism and Sexual Potential

While most people may readily acknowledge the importance of becoming and talent development as an essential part of abundant living in spiritual, educational, and social domains, they frequently struggle to see how this can also apply to sexuality. If someone wants to be an artist, a chef, or an athlete, most of us can appreciate the sense of accomplishment that he or she may find in developing and expressing those talents. In fact, when someone has a persistent desire to pursue certain experiences, we usually say that those passions are a core part of his or her identity and personality. We sometimes even describe ourselves and others according to such passions, such as "I *love* being a mother;" "he *is* an artist," "she just *comes alive* when she is teaching." Hopefully we can also appreciate the sense of loss, restlessness, and unhappiness when someone is unable to fully pursue their interests and reach their full potential.

But does the need for becoming apply to human sexuality? The answer to this is *yes*, even though we rarely think about sexual potential in this way. The primary reason for this may be that we do not fully acknowledge the significance of the sexual part of our divine nature—what we will call *eroticism*. Eroticism includes our innate and insistent sexual impulses and feelings. We typically experience our "erotic self" early in life as we begin to show interest in and curiosity about sex; this often leads to thoughts, excitement, dreams, and fantasies about sexual experiences. As our bodies mature, we become more aware that our body is able to experience remarkably heightened pleasures of touch and arousal. However, because these early experiences with sexual desire and eroticism are rarely talked about openly—let alone validated or encouraged—many of us may have grown up with a degree of uncertainty about whether our sexual desires and arousal patterns are something we should express or suppress in ourselves. Because of such mixed signals, many spouses later in marriage may still struggle to talk about their sexual desires, and are still uncertain how they should respond to their own and their partner's eroticism in marriage.

It bears mentioning that while our religious culture struggles to acknowledge sexual desire and eroticism in general, there seems to be a particular reluctance to acknowledge eroticism in women. Perhaps this comes from the modesty lessons given to young women that emphasize young men's reactions to the uncovered female form, or maybe it is because of the frequent cautions about pornography use among men; either way, many people seem to accept the myth that women do not have similar sexual desires and passions as men. A common perspective is that sex is something men "do to women," or something that men desire and women simply provide to men as some form of marital responsibility; another is that women enjoy the emotional closeness of sex, but do not share a similar passion as their husbands for the physical sensations of touch, arousal, and orgasm that accompany intense sexual experience. Such denials of female eroticism can create lasting confusion in young women as they experience their own eroticism while coming of age (having sexual thoughts, desires, and fantasies); yet while trying to make sense of these parts of themselves, they may be influenced to conclude that such passions are not womanly, motherly, or virtuous. Regretfully, such perspectives deny the shared reality of eroticism for both men and women; and when denied, creates distance between spouses; but when accepted, it can create unity and closeness.

Gospel Perspectives on Eroticism

Perhaps another reason why we may individually and collectively shun eroticism is that while growing up we were mistakenly led to link eroticism to temptation and transgression. We may see our sexual desires as "sensual" or even "devilish," thus, developing or intentionally pursuing these desires would be very inappropriate or excessive. Such thinking also falls into the traditional Christian philosophy that the physical body and its functions are corrupt, and must therefore be subdued and overcome by the spirit. Embracing sexual wholeness, however, helps us appreciate that the physical body is as divine as the spirit body, and that the fullness of our human nature includes developing the capacity of the body—as well as the spirit.

Comparing other forms of physically-based talent development such as dancing or athletics may be helpful here. We typically do not feel that it is inappropriate for someone with physical talents to steadily work at using their body to achieve athletic prowess; we would not discourage such a person from learning to express their deepest feelings through dance or some other physical form of artistic expression. In a similar way, we are all sexual beings with a divine potential or talent for erotic pleasure. To fully express and enjoy this pleasure with heaven's approbation, we have to first feel that we are doing something "worthwhile," and that such activity will build a relationship; and secondly, we have to become very familiar with our own bodies, much like an athlete who carefully develops the important muscles that contribute to athletic adeptness. While few of us will become world-class athletes, most of us can learn to play some sport with reasonable proficiency if we have the passion and if we practice. As an added bonus, athletes have often experience what is called *runner's high*; but no athletic activity has the added bonus of the orgasmic experience that can be enjoyed by couples who learn to be erotic.

Why Does Sexual Becoming Matter?

Let's revisit the story of one couple from the first chapter, and then meet a new couple. You may remember Alex who was concerned that his wife—who joined the church later in her life—was a little too liberal in her sexual expressions, and that she enjoyed sexual activities other than intercourse; he wanted to know what was allowable or appropriate in a sexual relationship. In our experience we have found two groups of people who may need to resurrect their eroticism. First are people like Alex who—often due to guilt inducing messages about their sexuality as adolescents, and poor sexual education from parents and leaders—are so worried about what is "right" that they do not allow their sexual feelings and desires to flourish and blossom in marriage. People like Alex seem to have had their eroticism smothered during adolescence. The second group are couples who may have begun their marriages with an erotic aspect to their relationship, but have largely lost their eroticism over time.

Aimee and Craig, who have been married for nine years, are an example of this second group. While their relationship was once vibrant and exciting, Craig now finds himself in the most demanding stage of his career, and Aimee is spending most of her energy with three young children, so now they are rarely sexual with each other. They get along fine and have never had much conflict; most of their conversations now center around their children's needs. The slow demise of their sexual relationship became most noticeable after the birth of their third child; there were some complications for Aimee, and her recovery was slow and difficult. Craig was as attentive to her as he could be, but he had recently been promoted and his boss was demanding more of his time.

Even after Aimee fully recovered, the addition of one more child seemed to make it much more difficult to keep family life in balance. And the sexual area of their relationship was overshadowed for both of them. On occasion Craig would initiate sex, but he could tell that Aimee wasn't really into it; she would sometimes make offhand remarks about just one more person needing her attention. Rather than fight for their relationship, Craig retreated. Later, when Aimee found herself feeling emotionally distant from Craig, she then tried to initiate sex, but found that Craig wasn't much interested. Curiously, they even began to refer to each other as *Mom* and *Dad*—further de-sexualizing their relationship. What Aimee and Craig may not realize is that the erotic aspect of their relationship is slowly dying; and that this important glue is weakening to the point where their relationship is becoming more and more fragile.

President Spencer W. Kimball said:

> *If you study the divorces, as we have had to do in these past years, you will find there are one, two, three, four reasons. Generally sex is the first. They did not get along sexually. They may not say that in the court. They may not even tell that to their attorneys, but that is the reason (The Teachings of Spencer W. Kimball, p. 329).*

What Aimee and Craig, as well as Alex and his wife, need is to resurrect their eroticism. But this will not be easy. In Alex's case, he is not even aware of what he is missing; and he will have to unlearn much of his sexual pre-conditioning—about which he is largely ignorant, and will thus be extra challenging. For Aimee and Craig, their lives have become so busy and child-centered that they will have to substantially change their paradigm about what matters most.

We are anxious to point out that while the word *erotic* has recently become asso-ciated with the pornography industry, where the adversary has hijacked its pure meaning and twisted it for his own schemes; its real roots are broader, deeper, and more noble than sexually arousing images. Erotic love is the sexual passionate love sanctioned within marriage. We contrast it with the filial or companionate love that is identified by feelings of friendship, or the charitable love that is associated with feelings of compassion. It is also important to note that erotic love is the more unique love in that it is designed to be explored and enjoyed only within marriage, whereas companionate and charitable love may be experienced both within and outside of marriage. So, if couples let their erotic love die through neglect, they are losing the type of love that may most uniquely define their relationship. And when that happens, they tend to become more like friends or roommates or siblings—rather than deeply intimate spouses and lovers.

It is true that the quality of a couple's sexual relationship is reflected in their sense of belonging, and that the quality of a couple's belonging is reflected in their sexual relationship. But it would be a mistake to assume that emotional connection and loving communication guarantee a satisfying sexual relationship. In fact, we have found that one of the problems with books on marital intimacy is that they often teach that if couples are emotionally intimate, they will automatically be sexually intimate. Our experience, however, shows that there are many couples who would rate their emotional intimacy as very satisfactory, yet who feel that their sexual relationship is not what they would like it to be; the fact that they have such a good relationship in other aspects makes their sexual dissatisfaction particularly disheartening. There is a sense that they could "have it all," so to speak, if they could just nurture a more satisfying sexual relationship.

Of course couples should set realistic expectations when it comes to how much excitement they should expect in marital sexuality. And sometimes sex may be more comforting and reassuring than exciting, and that is fine. Also, couples and families typically settle in to predictable patterns; most couples have daily or weekly habits of spending time together that may include watching a movie, going on a walk, doing a crossword puzzle, cooking a meal, or shopping. Sharing such activities of ordinary life can strengthen their relationship. However, if these habits become their only recreation pattern, then their time together may turn stale and become less satisfying. In time, they may just be going through the motions, adopting a pragmatic approach to spending time together (i.e., *it is just what we do*), but not really enjoying one another's company. Likewise, we inevitably feel a sense of loss or disappointment when sex becomes routine. Just as adding variety to how a couple spends time together by going on a hike, planning a surprise date night, or going on an overnight getaway, an added measure of creativity or novelty in marital sexuality can increase anticipation and heighten enjoyment of sexual experiences.

Also, although it is somewhat paradoxical, personal growth may be the genesis for creating such newness in a relationship. Granted, couples can become too comfortable—with their marriage, with themselves, and with their patterns of interaction; but growth and progression can cause people to change and expand; spouses develop a fuller sense of individuality; natural differences are accentuated. And these differences, when founded on a strong commitment to belonging, ironically create a newness and authenticity that can keep a marriage vibrant and energized. As Elder Bruce Hafen explains, "No true sense of belonging, religious or romantic, was ever intended to smother or submerge our sense of personal identity. Indeed, one of the most rewarding blessings of true belonging is that it can enrich so fully—even make possible—the process of each person's development toward personal fulfillment" (p. 62).

Becoming and Sexual Spark

We live in a time where *sexual chemistry* is a common topic of conversation; it is discussed in a somewhat mysterious way where couples cannot predict whether they will have it or not. Conventional wisdom in modern dating is that a couple either has it or they don't. But clearly this type of thinking can create problems, for it may encourage couples to have sex prior to marriage in order to test their sexual chemistry with each other. Other couples may feel the spark of sexual energy early in their relationship, but then see it fade. This may be the typical pattern if it is believed that the *spark* or *chemistry* in a couple's sex life is uncontrollable or unexplainable. Couples may then feel that it's time to search for sexual satisfaction and passion in another relationship.

Many young couples are told to "get real" about sex; that their naïve desires for a vital sexual relationship are unrealistic or immature—almost as if accepting a passionless marriage was a marker of maturity. So, what is the solution? The key is to recognize that sexual spark doesn't just happen, it is created; it is understandable and controllable. At its core, sexual spark is about sexual becoming, and developing a relationship where spouses can authentically explore their eroticism with each other; where spouses can share their inner desires with each other in both spoken and unspoken ways during sex. It also requires a mutual commitment to authenticity to share their desires—even if they are unsure how their spouse may react, or fear they may be rejected.

There are at least three main ingredients needed to develop and maintain sexual spark in a relationship: authenticity, creativity, and intensity. Some of these may naturally be present in new relationships but can wane over time; others develop over time as couples engage in the intimacy of confrontation, and authentic sexual expression and communication. Spouses should consider how well these facets of healthy eroticism describe themselves and their relationship.

Authenticity

While authenticity is discussed in more detail in Chapter 14, it is important to develop some of the ideas here. Sexual becoming is a developmental process fundamentally based in *authenticity*. When you are authentic, you strive to be open, real, and disclosing. Within marriage, authenticity involves sharing our private thoughts and desires, and includes two aspects: *self discovery* and *genuine disclosure*. Eroticism is an evolving part of each of us which we need to discover, since no one enters marriage knowing all of their sexual preferences or what will unlock their sexual potential. Furthermore, in instances like Alex, many people may enter marriage with significant liabilities in terms of their attitudes about sex. Thus each spouse discovers—and creates—his or her erotic self. Spouses should support one another in this sometimes sensitive and stressful process of self discovery, and be open to new experiences.

Additionally, spouses should commit to genuine disclosure to their partner both during and in between sexual experiences. Whether initiating or responding to sexual advances, spouses engage in a vulnerable dance that can result in feelings of acceptance or feelings of rejection—depending on how it is handled. These pivotal interactions can also highlight similarities or differences between spouses. So for those who struggle with the intimacy of confrontation, the possibility of feeling rejected—or the discovery of differences—may become threatening enough to cause them to retreat to the safer ground of predictable sexual interaction. Such a retreat may indeed reduce the potential of confrontation, but it will also inevitably lead to a loss of vitality and spark in the sexual relationship.

Creativity

One of the compelling reasons why couples should embrace authenticity is that the differences that may emerge from such a way of living can become the foundation of creativity—a key ingredient of erotic sexuality. This is easy to see in many couples who experience so much sexual energy during dating and early marriage; the newness of their interactions requires them to be creative. Whether it is the anticipation of holding hands for the first time, the excitement of kissing good night after a third date, or the exhilaration of sexual touch shared in the early weeks of marriage, the novelty of these experiences enhances the sexual spark of the relationship. In such emerging relationships most experiences with physical intimacy are surrounded by newness: unique settings, first experiences, diverse sensations, and heretofore unknown emotions.

Even though relationships cannot stay new forever, some of the features that are associated with early coupling can be perpetuated in a couple's ongoing relationship by being creative, and fostering unexpected pleasures in our marriage. If spouses want to break the predictability in their sexual patterns, they should let their partner know that they are carefully considering this facet of their relationship. This also conveys that sex is a valued part of the marriage and should make the spouse feel desirable and wanted. Another effective way to foster sexual creativity is for spouses to embrace their divinely endowed capacity for sexual fantasy, and to practice focusing their sexual thinking *into* their relationship rather than *away* from it. This *private* energy associated with erotic imagination can be funneled into *shared* sexual interactions.

Intensity

In many ways, this third ingredient of sexual spark is both a means and an end of embracing eroticism in marriage. When spouses are open to the process of sexual becoming, it will promote a relationship pattern that is marked by more intense and arousing sexual experiences (ends). But, we also encourage spouses to see intensity as a means to sexual spark. Intensity is not just about the arousal phase *during* sex, but should also include the excitement and anticipation we can cultivate *between* sexual experiences. Thus, healthy couples who foster eroticism in their marriage are not afraid to find ways to playfully share their interest in being sexual with each other. A striking difference between most dating couples and many married couples is that the daters flirt a lot more with each other, and find ways to let each other know that they are thinking about each other, and that they want to be together; too many married couples take their attraction to each other for granted, and the symbols of desire get muffled in their daily interactions. Intensity is often the fruit of skillful seduction—a worthwhile art that can be learned to entice one's spouse and awaken desire for sexual involvement. Therefore, spouses should make the principle of intensity a priority in their desiring, anticipating, planning, initiating, and responding to sexual experiences; this will foster the type of sexual spark that will allow both sexual becoming and belonging to flourish in their marriage.

So is there hope for Alex's relationship, or Aimee and Craig's? Definitely! Resurrecting eroticism is something that ought to be fun and exciting. And it isn't anywhere near as challenging as losing 30 pounds and keeping it off for the rest of your life. When we refer to eroticism, we are really talking about learning to do something that can result in much more attraction, closeness, more intense sexual experiences, and enduring relationship bonding—all of which are very rewarding outcomes.

While Alex, and Aimee and Craig need to use more authenticity, creativity, and intensity, their path to resurrecting eroticism will probably be quite different. For Alex, he has to first be authentic enough with himself to admit that he is a sexual being—and that is wonderful. To achieve this, however, he has the task of counteracting negative, guilt-inducing thoughts that may crop up in his head—thoughts that were largely planted by parents, other leaders, and maybe even his somewhat obsessive personality. If Alex's negative thinking is intractable and he finds that he cannot change it on his own, he would do well to seek help from a qualified cognitive therapist or marriage therapist, where he can learn to identify and substitute more appropriate cognitions and actions. Assuming he will eventually give himself permission to have sexual desires, fantasies, and feelings, he can then start to expand and enjoy his sexual self; he is fortunate to have a wife who is more erotically capable, and who can guide him into being more creative and intense. In many ways he just needs to relax, let go of fears, and allow his wife to lead him along into a place where they can experiment, play, and enjoy their bodies together.

As for Aimee and Craig, they have to be authentic enough to admit that even though they are busy, all of the reasons for why their eroticism is on life support, all of the rationalizing for why they have let this important area of their relationship die—are all just excuses. They will need to make some difficult, prayerful, and open commitments to each other, and to God, to never let anything else take priority over their marriage, and this includes keeping their sexual life vibrant and a dependable part of each week. They may also need to carve out time each week where in private, Aimee can rediscover her adult needs and desires—without the kids or Craig asking her for something. They may also need to formally schedule "erotic" evenings together where they can plan, talk, or tease each other about their fun upcoming night to enjoy uninterrupted sexual play and connection. They should accept that there will always be distractions when there are kids, church callings, job responsibilities, extended family, etc.; yet if their erotic needs are prioritized up to at least the same level as church attendance and family home evening, they will be taking a most important step toward ensuring a lasting and vibrant marriage.

Questions to Ponder

1. *How do I show that I am comfortable with the idea of eroticism?*

2. *How well do I know my own body?*

3. *Do I consider eroticism as womanly, motherly, and virtuous?*

4. *Am I a "roommate" or a "sibling" to my spouse, or am I a lover?*

5. *Do I feel desired in my relationship? Does my spouse feel desired?*

6. *How do I create a sexual spark in my marriage? What might I consider trying in the future?*

7. *Do differences with my spouse tend to threaten me or create an air of excitement? Why might I feel the way I do?*

8. *How can I make room for more intense sexuality in my life?*

7

THE PHYSICAL DIMENSION: ENHANCING SEXUAL STIMULATION

Created in the Image of God

If we are to properly understand the physical dimension of our sexual nature, we should first carefully consider the divine attributes we share with our Heavenly Parents. Each of us is a beloved spirit son or daughter of Heavenly Parents who was created in their image. As literal offspring of God, both our spirit bodies and our physical bodies have been created such that we are fully equipped to experience all that our loving Father in Heaven intended for us to experience in this life—which includes sexual pleasure and satisfaction. Because of this special capacity, a needed starting point for developing sexual wholeness is a sound knowledge of how husbands' and wives' bodies were designed to function sexually, and how to enhance the physical sensations experienced during sexual intimacy.

To discuss this topic requires a special reverence and sense of sacredness—particularly because our modern culture tends to reveal the human body in calculated ways meant to titillate and arouse self-indulgent attitudes about sex. Yet a respectful discussion of our bodies and the physical dimension of our sexuality should inspire an awe for the majesty of our Heavenly Parents, and a profound appreciation of the incredible physical bodies They have given us—bodies that have the capacity to experience great joy in this life, and a fullness of joy in the eternities to come.

Turning to the True Expert

An important part of developing a satisfying sexual relationship in marriage includes learning how to physically stimulate each other in arousing and pleasurable ways. But for many couples, including those who are committed to chastity during courtship, doubts about "knowing what to do" may create feelings of anxiety about sex. Even spouses who have been married for a while may want to increase the quality of physical stimulation experienced during sex.

In our sexually-fragmented society, a common solution offered in these situations is just to provide couples with "technique training" that focuses on sexual positions and specific sexual behaviors. The importance of such "technical proficiency" has been overblown by the popular media and in many sex manuals. Sadly, such "prescribed practices" reinforce the tradition that there are certain "right ways" to have sex, and that becoming proficient in those methods is necessary for satisfying sex. The truth, however, is that physical technique is helpful in the arousal process when it aligns with each spouse's physical body and personal preferences. Thus, learning about sexual techniques from the "experts" is of little value since their prescribed practices are sometimes contrary to the preferences of either spouse.

So the best person to teach you how to provide satisfying physical stimulation to your spouse—is your spouse! Optimal physical stimulation may be achieved only if spouses are willing to make known to each other their body sensations and sexual desires during sex. This requires a person to really want to be taught about their spouse's likes and dislikes, and then a willingness to change their behavior and respond to such preferences. As you can imagine, it includes both verbal and non-verbal communication, and requires spouses to be authentic and open with each other. Following this pattern during the actual sexual experience can have the long-term benefit of keeping spouses "in synch" with each other. We will discuss sexual communication and authenticity in more detail later in the section on the emotional dimensions of sexuality; but at this point it is sufficient to remember that there is only one sexual technique expert that you need to pay any attention to—your own spouse. He or she will be the best source from which to learn how to enhance the quality of sexual response in your relationship.

Even though the primary classroom for improving physical stimulation comes from within your own relationship, we have also found that couples can benefit by gaining a better understanding of how men's and women's bodies function sexually—their sexual physiology. Peter and Shelly, a newlywed couple, are a good example of how this may make a difference. During their time of dating and engagement, they developed a loving and close relationship and openly discussed their shared goal of being sexually pure as they entered marriage. Both of them love kissing each other and were looking forward to having sex with each other after their wedding. On their honeymoon, however, and in the following weeks, they found that sex was "not very good." Even though Peter was experiencing orgasm when they made love, Shelly was not becoming very aroused and so penetration was uncomfortable. Once Peter recognized this, he was embarrassed—and frustrated. Of course Peter and Shelly loved to be close to each other while undressed, but they were worried that they might not be "doing it right." A private conversation with Peter and Shelly quickly revealed that they were both lacking a basic understanding about how their bodies function sexually. Armed with new knowledge, Peter and Shelly then experimented with specific types of touch which noticeably improved their sexual experiences.

The Anatomy of the Sexual Response

Men's and women's bodies are divinely designed with a special capacity to experience sexual pleasure and satisfaction. Even as a fetus develops in the womb, it

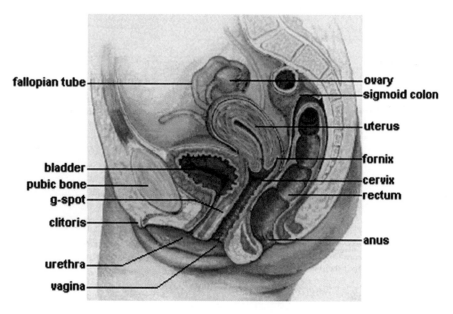

Figure 7.1 – Women's Sexual Anatomy

goes through a common phase of sexual development before it manifests itself as a male or a female child. During this initial phase, a cell mass develops which will eventually become the sexual organs of the fetus. We want to emphasize that the developmental foundation for the sexual organs of females is exactly the same as the developmental foundation for the sexual organs of males. It is during subsequent stages that the unique male or female anatomy emerges. Diagrams of women's and men's sexual anatomy are provided in Figures 7.1, 7.2, and 7.3. Study these diagrams to become familiar with the parts of men's and women's bodies that primarily contribute to sexual arousal and orgasm during sex.

It is widely known that the penis is the primary part of the male body designed to experience physical stimulation. However, one common misunderstanding for couples such as Peter and Shelly is the idea that a woman's vagina plays the same role in female stimulation and arousal. What many people don't know is that for women, the clitoris is usually the body part that plays the most critical role in sexual arousal and orgasm. Consider that the clitoris has the same number of nerve endings as does the penis—even though it is only one-tenth the size, thus making the clitoris more sensitive than any other part of either a male or female human body.

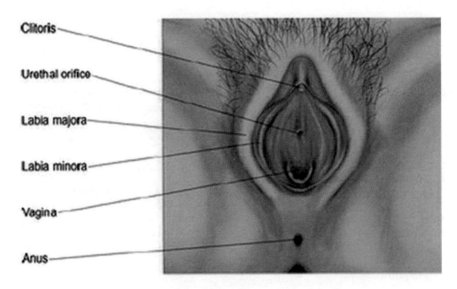

Figure 7.2 – Women's Sexual Anatomy

Even though vaginal stimulation does contribute to arousal in women, the walls of the vagina are not endowed with as many sensitive nerve endings as the clitoris. Peter and Shelly were not aware of the importance of the clitoris in female arousal, and so had naively developed a pattern of attempting intercourse without first stimulating clitoral arousal.

It is significant to understand that the clitoris has no other physical purpose than to provide physical arousal and pleasure for women. This should be additional and special evidence that God has created his children to fulfill divine purposes—which includes the capacity to experience sexual pleasure in marriage. Thus, for married couples, learning how to successfully stimulate the wife's clitoris is often necessary for her sexual fulfillment, and ultimately for the couple's sexual fulfillment. Proper arousal of a woman's clitoris often requires patience since the clitoris can be very sensitive; initially, it may require light or indirect stimulation. A husband should be very responsive to his wife as he helps her build her sexual arousal.

For men, the nerves that enhance arousal in the pelvic region are primarily in the penis; for women, however, there are typically three key areas that have

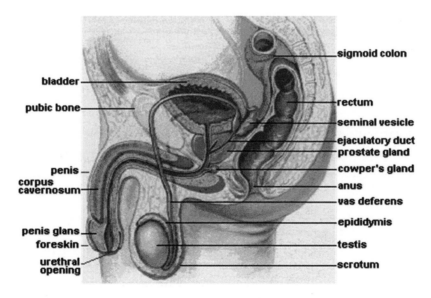

Figure 7.3 – Men's Sexual Anatomy

sufficient nerve endings to enhance arousal: the clitoris, which has the largest concentration of nerves, and different parts of the vagina, and the perineum (the area between the vagina and anus) also has clusters of nerves that can be very pleasurable when touched. Also keep in mind that each woman has her own unique grouping of nerves in these three areas, so there is no standard approach to touch and arousal that will fit all women. It will require some flexibility and some exploration for both partners to discover what areas of her pelvic region are more or less sensitive—some at even different stages in the arousal process. For instance, maybe early in the arousal process a particular woman prefers that her breasts are caressed, while at another stage she may prefer touch at the entrance of her vagina. By contrast, a different woman might prefer mostly clitoral stimulation. This can be a lighthearted and respectful process of exploration and discovery, especially if couples don't expect immediate "success" in terms of reaching climax quickly. Details regarding the opportunities that may be possible because of the unique physiological makeup of each woman will be discussed in Chapter 11.

Men's primary sexual arousal comes from stimulation of the penis. Keep in mind, though, that for both sexes other parts of the body can also be very responsive to sexual touch and stimulation. Our bodies have numerous "erogenous zones" with heightened sensitivity that can contribute to arousal and orgasm. As arousal progresses, changes in blood flow stimulate even more nerve endings, and thus further enhance sensations of touch throughout men's and women's entire bodies, not just in the local genital area. For example, kissing is often very arousing because lips and tongues have collections of nerve endings that are very sensitive and receptive to touch. Even parts of the head such as the neck, ears, and scalp are receptive to touch. The chest has a clustered network of nerves that make stimulation of the breasts and nipples a pleasurable experience for both men and women. Other parts of the body, including the stomach, the softer skin of the inner arms and thighs, and the nerve endings in the feet, may also be responsive to sensual touch.

The Psychology of the Sexual Response

The quality of *physical* stimulation during sex is one of two key components that will lead to arousal and orgasm. The other primary component is *psychological* stimulation, meaning the amount of desire, expectation, and excitement spouses have about being sexual with each other. Psychological stimulation may also be enhanced or limited by emotional and spiritual dimensions experienced during sex. So as we now consider those dimensions of sexual nature, we encourage you to view them as influencing our sexual responses.

Even though psychological stimulation is deeply influenced by emotions, it is still profoundly interconnected to the physical dimension of sexuality. This is because the single most important sexual organ for both women and men is the *brain*. What happens in our brains during sex is as much due to physical arousal as it is emotional or psychological arousal. So unless the brain becomes aroused biologically—and not just emotionally, the body typically will not become aroused enough to reach high levels of arousal and orgasm.

Fascinating research in recent years using sophisticated brain scanning technologies have helped us understand that sex is at least as much a brain experience as it is a body experience; the sexual response of the brain is as real as the sexual response of the rest of the body. The human brain is comprised of nerve cells called *neurons*, where thoughts, desires, sensations, and emotions are blended together and given meaning. Scientists refer to certain clusters of neurons as "pleasure centers" because these parts of the brain process the neurotransmitters (brain chemicals) that are associated with the pleasurable experiences of the body, including sexual arousal and orgasm.

One important neurotransmitter is dopamine. When we are pleasurably stimulated—by how we are touched, what we see, what we hear, or what we may smell—dopamine is activated in these pleasure centers of the brain, which then excites the cells to send this message to another part of the brain: "this feels good!" This shows that our minimum arousal level has been reached. When spouses reach their minimum orgasm thresholds, other brain chemicals such as oxytocin and vasopressin are activated. In women, oxytocin is released in the brain during orgasm and causes pleasurable genital contractions; in men, oxytocin is involved during male sexual response, and vasopressin is released during orgasm. It is meaningful to note that brain researchers believe that oxytocin and vasopressin are associated with increased feelings of trust, attachment, and bonding between sexual partners.

Understanding the important role the brain plays in physical arousal should help couples appreciate how the emotional aspects of their relationship can't help but affect their sexual relationship. For example, consider again the patterns of the couples that we described in Chapter One. Jenny is not only feeling emotionally distant from Steve, but other thoughts and feelings about their relationship are probably obstructing her brain's ability to be aroused, thus hampering the physical arousal of her body when they try to have sex. Alex may be experiencing less intensity of sexual response since he often worries about whether he and his wife are having the right kind of sex. For Shannon, her insecurities may cause her to worry about whether her husband finds her attractive enough during sex—yet another negative thought pattern that will likely reduce the amount of dopamine released in the brain.

Brain processes are very complex, and our current understanding of brain functioning is still growing. It should still be clear, though, that the sexual responses of our bodies are intertwined with changes in brain chemistry and functioning for better of for worse. Once we appreciate the pivotal role our brains play in our sexual response, we are much more likely to embrace the need for sexual wholeness; it helps highlight the need for sexual wholeness, and explains why the spiritual and emotional dimensions of our relationships must be integrated with the physical aspects of marital sexuality.

Questions to Ponder:
1. *Am I becoming an expert on my spouse's preferred physical stimulation?*
2. *Is my spouse becoming an expert on my preferred physical stimulation?*
3. *How do we allow—and encourage—this to happen?*
4. *Do I understand the function of the clitoris?*
5. *Have I discovered the types of touch that stimulate my/my wife's clitoris?*
4. *How can I psychologically stimulate my spouse?*

8

THE PHYSICAL DIMENSION:
SEXUAL RESPONSE THRESHOLDS

Since the 1960s, most therapists and health educators have taught that sexual experiences should be understood using a model called the "sexual response cycle." Several versions have been developed over the years. These models separate sexual experience into phases or stages, and just focus on *physical changes* in the genital system and certain parts of the body. The sexual response cycle has even become the foundation for classifying sexual dysfunctions—based only on these physical phases (e.g., desire disorders, arousal disorders, orgasm disorders, etc.). This focus on stage models has had a tremendous impact on how our modern society perceives sexual functioning, health, and intimacy. In fact, phase models of sexual response have become so common in sex education that they are usually accepted as undisputed truths of human sexual experience. Couple sex books often teach about the "sexual response cycle" as if it were biological fact rather than a conceptual model. Given their prevalence, we want to give an overview of such phase models, and then examine the strengths and weakness of viewing sexual response strictly through this lens.

Traditional Phase Models

Most models of the sexual response cycle include four primary phases: a desire phase, an arousal phase, an orgasm phase, and a resolution phase.

1. The Desire Phase

Phase models of sexual response typically define *sexual desire* as strong emotional urges to initiate and respond to sexual stimulation. This view is consistent with popular notions of "libido," "sex drive," or "horniness," where people have a sexual energy that must be either expressed or suppressed. Due to a lack of physical markers (noticeable changes of the body), or biological indicators (traceable changes within the body), the "desire phase" has been the least explained stage in most phase models of sexual response. Rather than explaining what sexual desire really is, or where it may come from, most phase models simply accept sexual desire as innate, and thus needs no further explanation. Therefore, many educators who use phase models tend to emphasize that desire is almost an unimaginably complex phenomenon, and turn their attention to discussing factors that influence the level of desire in a relationship (e.g., biology, past experiences, current marital dynamics, among others).

2. The Arousal Phase

Most phase models teach that the desire phase is followed by an excitement or arousal phase. The basic idea is that when sexual desire is accompanied by stimulating thoughts or actual physical sensations, this leads to physical arousal and predictable changes in our bodies. The changes are most noticeable in the genital area, even though other areas of the body such as the breasts are also affected. The primary physiologic event that occurs during sexual arousal is called *vasocongestion*, where the veins of the pelvis dilate and fill with blood. These vascular changes enlarge the genital organs and produce sensations of tension, fullness, and warmth. In men, sexual arousal results in an increase in the rigidity, length, and circumference of the penis; in women, it leads to an enlargement of the vaginal canal, and the vagina becomes lubricated through the secretion of vaginal fluid. This process prepares men's and women's bodies for sexual intercourse and orgasm.

3. The Orgasm or Climax Phase

Phase models next emphasize that arousal builds toward the climax of orgasm. At the climactic moment that marks the orgasm phase, all of the tension that has been built up in the pelvis area due to vasocongestion is suddenly released in a series of contractions involving muscles of the internal and external sexual organs. Simultaneously, the extra blood that has collected in the veins of the pelvis is released to flow back into the body. Women experience a series of involuntary rhythmic contractions in the genital area; in men, orgasm results in the involuntary ejaculation of semen in a series of rhythmic contractions. The contractions of orgasm produce remarkable feelings of intense physical pleasure.

4. The Resolution or Afterglow Phase

Following orgasm, some phase models note that sexual arousal slowly abates and bodily processes return to pre-arousal states. This process is called the resolution or afterglow phase. Some phase models ignore this process altogether, or if they do mention it, they do not sanction it as a phase.

Shortcomings in Phase Models

The biological processes described in phase models such as vasocongestion and orgasm are accurately described, and as we previously discussed in Chapter Seven, they are a valuable part of understanding sexual response and functioning. Nevertheless, any benefits that may be gained from learning about these biological processes will be significantly counteracted if they are not connected to the spiritual and emotional aspects of sex. In fact, when presented in isolation, phase models will likely promote two myths about marital sexuality:

Myth #1: There is only one right way to have sex

Orgasm is often portrayed as the goal of sex and the primary marker of sexual quality. Far too many couples become fixated on orgasm, believing that the presence and frequency of orgasms is validation—or lack thereof—that they have a good sex life. Even though sexually mature couples value physical arousal and orgasm in their relationship, they understand that marital closeness can also be strengthened by sexuality that does not involve orgasm. This myth was one of the stumbling blocks for Peter and Shelly, the couple whom we introduced in Chapter Seven. Much of their concerns about "not doing it right" stemmed from a misguided belief that orgasm was the only indicator of "good sex." In some sexual encounters, spouses may want to share mutual arousal and orgasm; but they needed to realize that there will be other times where rich intimacy can be fostered where only one spouse has an orgasm, or where neither one has an orgasm. When *intimacy*—rather than *orgasm*—is the prime focus of the experience, couples will be more open to a broad range of sexual expression in the course of their marriage, and reject the myth that there is only one right way to be sexual.

Myth #2: Sexual Arousal is Simultaneous

Almost without exception, phase models describe the process of only one person progressing through the phases of desire, arousal, and orgasm; there is rarely a discussion of two people being present in the experience. Also eliminated is the common pattern of husbands' and wives' progressing through the phases with different pace, intensity, and completion. Peter and Shelly did not fully appreciate how different their pace of arousal was from each other; they were proceeding at Peter's faster pace of arousal, but would have been better served to follow Shelly's slower pace. Once they understood that men's and women's sexual responses are naturally different, they were then able to thoughtfully respond to those differences.

The Sexual Response of Our Souls

Phase models can create as many problems as they solve because they fail to combine the emotional aspects of sexuality with the physical response of our bodies. They do not incorporate the human capacity for true intimacy, nor the profound emotional meanings that accompany sexual experience. As we have been emphasizing, to be sexually whole couples must appreciate that sexual response is determined by two key components: physical stimulation and psychological stimulation. *Physical stimulation* is the amount of "external stimulation" experienced during sex, and is a function of the quality and quantity of physical touch, as well as the body's capacity to process it. *Psychological stimulation* is "internal stimulation" and includes the emotions and thoughts spouses have during sex, and is also influenced by spouses' attitudes about sexuality and the quality of their overall relationship. Physical stimulation and psychological stimulation combine to create the *total level of stimulation* experienced in a given sexual encounter.

We should always integrate physical and psychological stimulation in our view of sexual response; couples will see that both physical and emotional "inputs" always are involved in creating the total level of stimulation experienced by each spouse during sex (see figure 8.1).

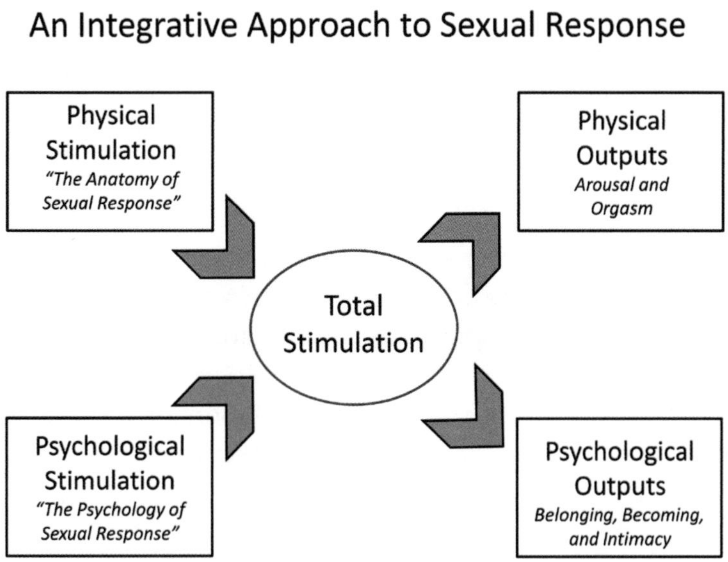

An Integrative Approach to Sexual Response

Figure 8.1 – An Integrative Approach to Sexual Response

This integrative approach also encourages us to pay careful attention to the physical and psychological "outputs" of sexual experiences as well. Even though the *physical outputs* (whether arousal and orgasm are experienced) may be readily apparent, the *psychological outputs* (whether intimacy was enhanced) is much less obvious but is much more important to a couple's overall relationship. When spouses attend to the physical aspects of sex, they should see improvements in the physical stimulation (input) and physical response (output) in their relationship; and when they attend to the spiritual and emotional dimensions of sexuality, they should see improvements in the psychological stimulation (input) and psychological response (output) in their marriage. This can become a virtuous circle of progression and joy.

Sexual Response Thresholds

Over the last several years, we have become convinced that teaching couples about sexual response *thresholds* is much more helpful than teaching them a sexual response *cycle*. On the cellular level, the body sends electrical impulses from specialized "sensors" to specialized "receptors." When the combined levels of physical and psychological stimulation reach "threshold sensitivity levels," certain physical changes and processes associated with sexual functioning automatically occur. Specifically, once the *arousal threshold* is reached, increased blood flow to the genital region produces erection in men and vaginal lubrication in women. Furthermore, once the *orgasmic threshold* is reached, the body triggers the release of built-up tension, genital contractions, and sensations of physical pleasure.

It is important to understand that these two stimulus thresholds for sexual response will vary, and are typically different between spouses. As we have learned, phase-based models of sexual response depict that arousal and orgasm is similar for all people; but a threshold perspective helps us appreciate that some people may have relatively low or high thresholds for arousal and orgasm, and that even these threshold levels can change for a given individual over time.

We note that most men have lower arousal and orgasmic thresholds than women, although this is not always the case. Additionally, thresholds may temporarily fluctuate due to fatigue, illness, medicines, hormonal changes, or other factors that can influence the body's ability to receive or process physical and psychological stimulation. Long-term patterns of threshold change are seen in the process of aging. Even then, there is growing evidence that like other physical processes, sexual response thresholds can also be conditioned—at almost any age; depending on the type of conditioning, our capacity for sexual stimulation will either increase or diminish.

Understanding each other's sexual response thresholds also helps us differentiate between psychological arousal and genital response. On the one hand, it is quite possible for a spouse to want sexual contact and feel aroused (i.e., psychological stimulation), even though their total stimulation has not yet reached their arousal threshold (and so there is no genital response yet). This experience may cause one spouse to question the other's sexual interest and ability, and may even stir some anxiety where one partner sees themselves as unattractive or undesirable by the other. On the other hand, the opposite can also occur, where a person may have an adequate genital response, but have minimal psychological stimulation. Rather than viewing genital response as the only indicator of whether someone is aroused, genital response should be seen as an indicator of a particular *level* of arousal— which may or may not be above their personal sensitivity threshold.

There is also a dynamic nature to sexual response. Variations in the amount and cadence of physical and psychological stimulation—during one sexual encounter—

affect sexual responses. For example, total stimulation may fluctuate above and below the arousal threshold within a given sexual encounter to where a husband may lose and gain an erection several times, or a wife may not have constant vaginal lubrication. Total stimulation may be sufficient to reach—intermittently—a spouse's personal arousal threshold, but not their orgasmic threshold. Stimulation that causes either rapid or delayed progression can be beneficial—or problematic—depending on whether a couple understands the key principles of sexual response thresholds.

Questions to Ponder:
1. *How well do I understand the psychological and physical sexual responses of my partner?*

2. *Does my spouse usually have high or low threshold levels? What are my own threshold levels?*

3. *How well do I understand my own stimulation, arousal and orgasm thresholds?*

4. *Do I feel that orgasm needs to be simultaneous for both husband and wife?*

9

THE PHYSICAL DIMENSION:
SEXUAL STATES AND TYPES OF INTIMACY

As spouses develop an awareness of their own and their partner's sexual thresholds, they will be better able to create mutually fulfilling sexual experiences. It is important to note that even though such sexual *awareness* can be partly acquired by knowledge of sexual functioning and different types of intimacy, the fullest development of this attribute will come through intimate sexual experience with your spouse. This ongoing process of developing an awareness of each other's sexual states and preferences is based on the principles of open disclosure and responsiveness.

Sexual States and Fostering Intimacy

As we noted previously, intimacy is best seen as a process—not an outcome. We continue to encourage you to define intimacy as a process of authentic disclosure, where you and your spouse share personal feelings, thoughts, desires, and experiences with each other. If couples keep this construct in mind, they will see that genuine closeness can be had through a variety of intimate experiences—only some of which will be physical—and only some of those will involve sexual arousal and orgasm. Sexually healthy couples cultivate a broad range of intimate experiences, where each type of intimacy is shared to the degree and frequency that fulfills each other's wants and needs.

As we discussed in Chapter Eight, both men's and women's bodies have two distinct response thresholds associated with sexual response: an arousal threshold and an orgasm threshold, where once reached, they enter into different states of physical arousal (i.e., aroused genitals, heightened sensitivity to touch), and psychological arousal (i.e., altered brain chemistry, heightened desire for touch, losing oneself in the experience, etc.). Spouses are therefore in one of three sexual states: a *non-aroused state* (below their arousal threshold); an *aroused state* (at least at their arousal threshold but below their orgasm threshold); or an *orgasmic state* (having reached their orgasm threshold). We will explain how spouses can engage in different types of personal disclosure in each of these sexual states, and experience unique types of vulnerability; this will create new ways to enhance intimacy.

Non-Arousing Intimacy

In this book, we have described in detail marital interactions of physical intimacy involving arousal and orgasm. Even though this is what most people label as "sex," we should always remember experiences with arousal and orgasm can never escape the influence of emotional and affectionate intimacy. That is an absolute truth for all people. We affirm that a divine purpose of sexual intimacy is to unify spouses and strengthen the marital bond—not just provide physical gratification. Therefore, we should define sexuality in whole terms that include both emotional and physical forms of intimate expressions. Intimacy is really "shared vulnerability," where people reveal themselves to each other, feel understood, and are hopefully nurtured in the interaction. This can happen when we talk, share, or disclose to others, as well as when we are physically close to them. So, when we talk about cultivating intimacy, we should think about broad behaviors—not just the physical behaviors typically defined as "sex."

Non-arousing intimacy is where spouses disclose emotional parts of themselves, with or without non-arousing touch. When spouses verbally share their feelings, ideas, opinions, or preferences with each other, they are fostering this type of intimacy. These conversations can be validating or confronting in nature; if they are done with kindness and understanding, they can strengthen feelings of trust, support, and security between spouses.

Spouses can also share non-arousing intimacy in physical ways by holding hands, sitting close to each other, cuddling while falling asleep, or affectionate kissing. Sometimes this happens during a conversation, or it may happen without talking at all. It is natural and appropriate for expressions of non-arousing intimacy to be part of a committed dating relationship. While typically started in dating, non-arousing intimacy should continue to play an important role in marriage. A common blunder made by some marriage partners—particularly young husbands—is to believe that arousing expressions of intimacy *replace* the non-arousing intimacy of dating. In sexually whole marriages, this is not the case; arousing intimacy is *added* to the foundation of non-arousing intimacy begun in dating, and naturally continues in marriage.

Arousing Intimacy

Physical and emotional closeness that triggers sexual thresholds creates a unique opportunity for spouses to interact with each other in their aroused and orgasmic sexual states. *Arousing intimacy* includes any kind of physical touch that activates a spouse's arousal threshold; it sets in motion powerful changes in their vascular system, respiratory system, nervous system, and brain functioning. Arousing intimacy is any form of physical touch that one or both spouses find stimulating, such as body massage, passionate kissing, or genital stimulation.

Orgasmic Intimacy

Orgasmic intimacy is any type of physical touch that activates a spouse's orgasm threshold. This threshold operates in much the same way as the arousal threshold; with sufficient stimulation, the body triggers the orgasm response, that brings a pleasurable release of built-up vascular tension, genital contractions, and feelings of warmth and contentment. These changes create a unique environment for self expression and disclosure. It is also a special opportunity for spouses to express acceptance, responsiveness, and love.

Even though arousing behaviors are often referred to as "foreplay," this term tends to imply that the only function of arousing intimacy is to move a couple toward orgasm. Obviously, most want their arousing intimacy to be "foreplay" that leads to orgasm; sexually healthy couples, however, also see arousing intimacy as a delightful type of intimacy in and of itself. While sexually healthy couples learn how to share regular orgasmic intimacy, they also understand that belonging and becoming can be strengthened in the aroused sexual state—even if it does not lead to orgasm for one or both partners. In fact, many spouses report that they enjoy the pleasures of arousing intimacy at least as much—or more than—they enjoy the pleasure of orgasm.

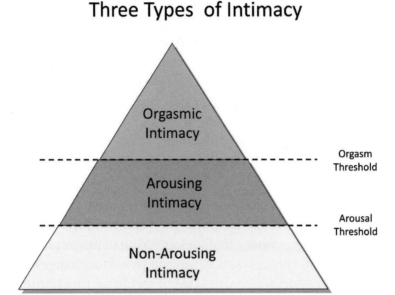

Three Types of Intimacy

Figure 9.1 – Sexual States and Types of Intimacy

As portrayed in Figure 9.1, non-arousing intimacy is a symbolic foundation upon which arousing intimacy and orgasmic intimacy can be built. Spouses tend to have personal preferences for the amount or ratio of each type of intimacy they would like to experience in their marriage. Remember that while spouses are often in the same sexual state at the same time, nearly all couples will also have encounters where they may be in different sexual states at a given time.

Congruent and Incongruent Sexual Experiences

As previously mentioned, phase models of sexuality usually portray intimacy as a process that happens the same for each member of the dyad, as shown in Figure 9.2, where there are only two thresholds. Sexually whole couples, however, appreciate that there are really four thresholds, as depicted in Figure 9.3: a wife's arousal threshold and orgasm threshold, and a husband's arousal threshold and orgasm threshold. They also appreciate that spouses typically experience sexual arousal with different pace, intensity, and completion. Figure 9.3 also illustrates that it is common for husbands to have lower or faster thresholds of arousal and orgasm than their wives; but this is not always the case—particularly in a specific interac-

Typical Portrayal of Sexual Response

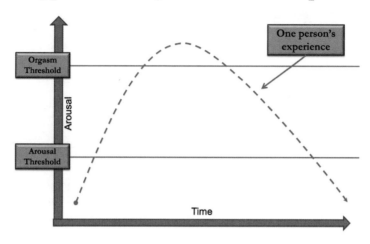

Figure 9.2 – Typical Phase Model Portrayal of Sexual Response

Four Sexual Response Thresholds

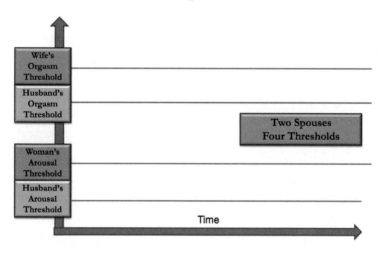

Figure 9.3 – A Threshold Model Portrayal of Sexual Response in Marriage

tion. Even though personal thresholds may vary from one episode to another (due to changing levels of psychological and physical stimulation), sexual thresholds for most couples are relatively predictable and stable.

While most congruent sexual experiences where spouses reach similar levels of arousal and sexual states are seen as fulfilling, satisfaction with *incongruent sexual experiences* will depend on personal expectations and the overall sexual pattern of the relationship. We encourage spouses to focus on overall relationship patterns, and avoid placing too much emphasis on individual sexual episodes. It is usually healthy for spouses to desire and experience orgasm on a regular basis; however, we have seen some couples struggle if they expect an orgasm in every sexual encounter. This creates unnecessary anxiety and may cause spouses to overlook the great benefits that come from non-arousing and arousing forms of intimacy. If intimacy—rather than orgasm—is their expectation, couples may be pleasantly surprised by the breadth of sexual interactions they can share over the years of their marriage.

We have found it to be enlightening to have couples draw graphs that represent common sexual experiences in their marriage. This usually stimulates a rich dialogue about shared or misunderstood parts of their sexual relationship. Each spouse plots their sexual states for a specific encounter, or pattern of encounters. The wife's experience is a red line, and the husband's experience is a blue line. We conclude this chapter by sharing some example graphs that depict what is common and desirable in marriage. These are just illustrative, and are not meant to be comprehensive.

Congruent Affectionate Intimacy

Figure 9.4 displays a couple's experience with congruent affectionate (non-arousing) intimacy. Notice how neither spouse reaches their arousal threshold. Affectionate intimacy is sometimes brief in its expression, such as kissing a spouse when he or she comes home, or holding hands, or the famous Mormon back rub in church! However, other expressions of non-arousing intimacy can be more prolonged, pleasurable, and bonding, such as a foot massage with lotion, or cuddling while watching a movie on the couch. Such interactions are also opportunities for emotional disclosure as couples converse while sharing these forms of non-arousing touch. Not surprisingly, non-arousing intimacy sometimes "gets

Congruent Non-Arousing Intimacy

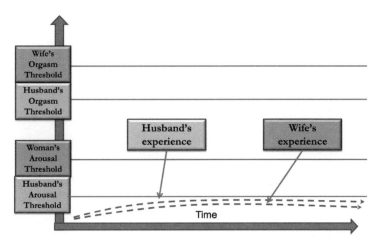

Figure 9.4 – Congruent Non-Arousing Intimacy

Congruent Arousing Intimacy

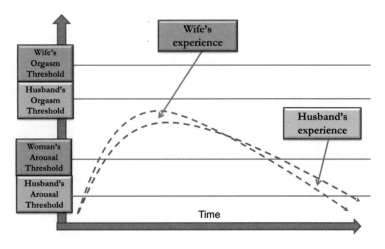

Figure 9.5 – Congruent Arousing Intimacy

things going" and shifts into arousing interactions; at any rate, spouses see non-arousing intimacy as a satisfying experience by itself.

Congruent Arousing Intimacy

In figure 9.5, notice how both spouses cross their arousal thresholds, but neither experiences orgasm; this is an example of *congruent arousing intimacy*. Depending on the amount of time that passes, this could represent either a brief—but intense—episode of passionate kissing, or a prolonged and erotic encounter where both spouses become very aroused. If we mistakenly call such arousal-only experiences *foreplay*, we may miss out on some deeply fulfilling rendezvous of prolonged sexual stimulation and experimentation; couples can avoid missing out by placing a higher priority on sometimes sharing arousing intimacy for its own sake. Many couples can deepen bonds by attending to the arousing intimacy part of their marriage, learning to enjoy the journey and worrying less about the destination.

Incongruent Orgasmic/Arousing Intimacy

Do you remember Joshua from Chapter One? He was the young husband who was surprised to learn at a marriage enrichment seminar that almost 40 percent of all women have a difficult time reaching orgasm through sexual intercourse alone, and that wives usually take at least four times longer than their husbands to reach orgasm. Joshua also learned that he may be experiencing premature ejaculation during sex with his wife. His wife was kind about these matters, but he was convinced that she was not enjoying sex as much as she could. Joshua was also concerned because they were having incongruent sexual experiences, where he was reaching his orgasm threshold but she was not. However, we don't know if this is a typical pattern in their sexual experiences, or if it only occurs infrequently.

Perhaps no pattern of sexual intimacy has received more attention than what we term *incongruent orgasmic/arousing intimacy* (see Figure 9.6), where the husband, like Joshua, experiences orgasm, but the wife does not. When viewed through the lens of traditional phase models of sexual response, this pattern represents sexual failure, selfishness, or both. Most couples enter marriage having heard of premature ejaculation, and most young husbands have a certain amount of anxiety about whether their sexual performance will be good enough to help their wife experience orgasm. Images of embarrassed husbands and dissatisfied wives abound—typically associated with this type of "lopsided" encounter. What such

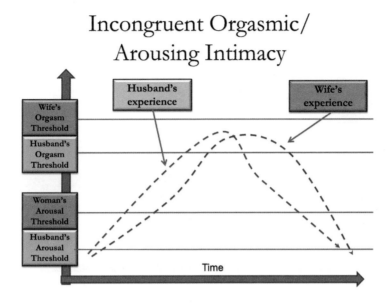

9.6 – Incongruent Orgasmic/Arousing Intimacy

perspectives fail to acknowledge, however, is that sexual encounters where a wife becomes aroused and the husband reaches orgasm are common to most marriages, and interestingly, are even a desired part of many couples' sexual repertoire.

Desire, preference, and expectation are key factors in determining satisfaction with this type of intimacy. Ratio or balance is another determining factor. So if Joshua's wife desired an orgasm but did not have one in a specific encounter, that is quite different from if she rarely has an orgasm over the course of many encounters; in the latter case then, this intimacy pattern may become dissatisfying and discouraging. And of course premature ejaculation can also cause problems (which issue we will discuss in Chapter 24). Nevertheless, when incongruent orgasmic/arousing intimacy is desired, and balanced with subsequent encounters that do involve orgasm, it can be a highly desirable form of marital intimacy. Even though many women do not readily have orgasms from just having intercourse with their husbands, both spouses find that they still enjoy the face-to-face closeness that comes with certain positions of intercourse. Such episodes may often include passionate kissing and emotional communion by looking into each other's eyes and talking with each other. It would be most unfortunate if couples were to view such personal and close times of bonding as a failure.

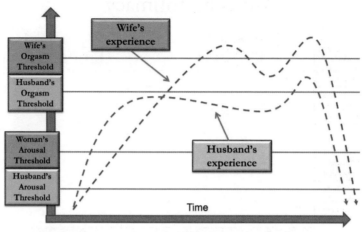

Figure 9.7 – Congruent Orgasmic Intimacy

Congruent Orgasmic Intimacy

Phase models of sexual response hold up congruent orgasmic intimacy as the ideal (see Figure 9.7). Even though we have said that several forms of sexual intimacy can be important to your relationship, we do not wish to imply that encounters where both spouses experience orgasm are not also important. In fact, given the emphasis on shared orgasm in our culture, it is understandable that this may even have a symbolic value for some couples. Also remember that the brain and body responses that come with orgasm are closely associated with feelings of trust and bonding for helpmates. There is also a growing and remarkable corpus of research that is discovering significant physical health benefits for men and women who have regular orgasms. Carefully consider both the subjective and objective reasons for why regular orgasmic intimacy that fits spouses' desires is an essential part of a wholesome intimate marriage.

With orgasmic intimacy, one problem that can arise by using phase models of sexual response is that they put a high premium on "simultaneous orgasm," where a husband and wife cross their orgasm thresholds at the same time. While such experiences of a "shared climax" are possible, and desirable, they may not be nearly as common as other patterns of congruent orgasmic intimacy, particularly for newly married couples. Most sexual advice encourages a "foreplay pattern" to mutual orgasm where arousing intimacy is first focused on the spouse with the higher threshold—typically the wife. This is what some call the "ladies first approach," where by design, the wife has an orgasm first—and that, often through stimulation other than intercourse; the husband then has an orgasm through intercourse or other forms of stimulation.

Besides a foreplay pattern, there is also an "afterplay pattern" of congruent orgasmic intimacy. Whether on purpose or not, a husband may cross his orgasm threshold before his wife has reached a high level of arousal or orgasm. But a husband's orgasm does not mean that their sexual encounter has to stop. If the wife wants to still have an orgasm, her husband should be responsive and continue to stimulate her in arousing ways. After the husband has an orgasm, there is a period of time in which he cannot become aroused enough to have another erection (called the *refractory period*); for many husbands, this is relatively short-lived as he finds himself able to become aroused again after several minutes of ongoing afterplay. For some husbands, particularly younger ones, they may find that they have "more control" with a second erection, and are then able to engage in more prolonged intercourse with their partner. If spouses will do their best to be responsive to each other, they can find special ways to make each intimate encounter—as well as their overall sexual relationship—a wondrous part of their married life.

Questions to Ponder:

1. *How aware am I of my spouse's thresholds? Do I understand how to help him/her pass their emotional and physical thresholds?*

2. *How well do proportions in the intimacy pyramid reflect the proportions of intimacy in my relationship? Do I have a strong enough base of emotional intimacy to support orgasmic intimacy?*

3. *Does arousing intimacy always lead to orgasmic intimacy? When it doesn't, how do I handle this within the relationship?*

4. *Do I discuss with my spouse his/her satisfaction with respect to each level of intimacy?*

10

THE PHYSICAL DIMENSION: COMMON SEXUAL DIFFERENCES

While a good measure of similarity is needed in a partnership like marriage, the amount of similarity may not always be the best indicator of a good fit or a well-formed relationship. In fact, an expectation for too much "sameness" usually indicates immature or unrealistic expectations in dating and marriage. Elder Merrill J. Bateman stated, "Men and women complement [not *compliment*] each other not only physically, but also emotionally and spiritually…. Men and women have different strengths and weaknesses, and marriage is a synergistic relationship in which spiritual growth is enhanced because of differences" (*Eternal Marriage*, p. 65). Differences in marriage—including sexual differences—are natural because we are all unique; they also come from growing up in different families, and from dating histories that shape in each spouse their own set of values, priorities, and ways of thinking about sex. With this reality in mind, we want to share some of the more common sexual differences between spouses in marriage. This may help couples see their own differences as quite normal, and better appreciate the ingenious complementary nature of marital sex.

Sexual Desire Differences

Perhaps the most common sexual difference between spouses is in the desired frequency of sexual intimacy. It is very common for one spouse to have a noticeably stronger desire for sexual stimulation than their spouse. This influences expectations for how often couples will have sex. Research shows that husbands typically desire sex more frequently than their wives; sometimes this pattern is reversed, with the wife having the higher desire. Even then, the labels *lower desire spouse* or *higher desire spouse* pattern are sometimes just a simple difference in how often spouses prefer to have sex, it can be easily misconstrued. Differences in desire are all too often the *fruit*, rather than the *root* of other less obvious but meaningful differences in spouses' sexual expectations. Let's discuss a few of these common misconceptions.

Desires for Different Types of Intimacy

When spouses report having a "desire difference," they are usually referring to the *amount* of sex each one wants to have each week or each month. What they may really be experiencing, however, is a difference in the *type* of intimacy they prefer. We discussed in Chapter Nine various types of intimacy, including non-arousing, arousing, and orgasmic intimacy; husbands and wives usually have their own expectations of how often they would like to experience each type of intimacy. Some may place a higher value on emotional or non-arousing forms of intimacy, enjoying conversations and shared time together. Others may favor non-arousing physical intimacy that is focused on things other than stimulating sexual arousal, such as holding hands, cuddling, or kissing. Still others may fancy arousing and orgasmic intimacy, along with its special afterglow. Most people value all types of intimacy in marriage to some degree, but they differ in how much they want of each type. If your goal is to cultivate sexual unity in your marriage, carefully learn about and be responsive to these intimacy desires of your partner.

So-called "frequency differences" can go both ways—it just depends on which spouse you are referring to. So a husband may claim that there is not enough arousing and orgasmic intimacy in the marriage, but his wife may counter that there is not enough non-arousing intimacy in the relationship—just like Jenny and Steve from Chapter One. Likewise, it is not uncommon that when a wife is troubled by the infrequency of orgasmic intimacy, her husband may be wishing that they could be more emotionally close. As we can see, both spouses are the "higher desire" spouse, and both are the "lower desire" spouse—it just depends on which type of intimacy you are referring to.

Sequence of Arousal

Some desire differences may result from the fact that some people experience sexual response in a different sequence than what is outlined in the traditional sexual response cycle. Traditional phase models purport that sexual desire *precedes* sexual arousal; new research suggests, however, that some spouses won't have a desire for sexual contact until *after* they have begun the arousal process. Sex therapist Dr. Michelle Weiner-Davis explains:

> *Some experts are beginning to question this one-size-fits-all perspective on sexual desire. They've noticed that for some people, sexual desire— the urge to become sexual—doesn't precede feeling aroused; it actually follows it. In other words, some people rarely (or never) find themselves fantasizing about sex or feeling sexual urges, but when they're open to becoming sexual with their spouses anyway, they often find the sexual stimulation pleasurable, and they become aroused. Once aroused, there is desire to continue. And that's every bit as much "sexual desire" as the more traditional view of things (*The Sex Starved Marriage, p. 12*).*

What this means is that in some marriages one spouse may be more-easily aroused either visually or psychologically, thus creating a quicker initial desire for sexual closeness; and the other spouse may be aroused primarily by physical touch and closeness. If such predispositions are not recognized, it can lead to misunderstandings and hurt feelings. A husband may feel rejected or hurt by his wife's initial lack of interest in sex—for "not being in the mood"—which he might interpret as not being interested in him; a wife may feel objectified, or obligated to respond to her husband's fast moves, unfairly labeling him as "only wanting one thing." The key to this conundrum is to remember that no one chooses his or her sequence of sexual arousal; it is innate. Once we become aware of these personal biases, we can shape a satisfying sexual relationship around them, rather than trying to change each other's approach to sex. You will soon find that nothing is as sexy and arousing as a caring and responsive spouse!

Low Sexual Desire

We have been discussing differences in preferences and priorities; we will now address the situation where one spouse has little or no interest in sex at all— regardless of type or frequency. Complaints about sexual desire are the primary problem brought to sex therapists. It is estimated that one out of three couples will struggle with differences stemming from sustained low sexual desire at some point in their marriage. Some studies show that nearly one in five married couples have sex fewer than ten times a year. If you think that low sexual desire is just a "wife problem," you may be buying into the myth that men are always more interested in sex than women. Dr. Weiner-Davis notes, however, that perhaps the best kept secret in America is low sexual desire in men, reminding us that women are not the only ones with this problem.

Sex is a crucial part of a couple's relationship because it offers couples the opportunity to give and receive pleasure, to connect emotionally, and forge bonds of togetherness. It is sex that defines a marriage as different from all other outside relationships. Because of this basic fact, a complete lack of desire for any sexual contact is likely to become a serious problem in a marriage. Having different sexual preferences is one thing; having no sexual preferences is quite another. We will discuss in depth how couples can address struggles related to low sexual desire in Chapters 22 and 23.

Sexual Practice Differences

Some couples have different preferences for certain sexual practices or behaviors. While these may be interlaced with differences of frequency or desire, it is instructive to consider them as a distinct type of sexual difference. For example, one spouse may want to experiment with new ways of sexual stimulation, whereas the other spouse may be rather satisfied with the status quo. As we discussed in Chapter Six, sexual creativity and variety differ between people, and such aspects of becoming are naturally reflected in the styles of sexual behavior that each spouse adopts to create an exciting and satisfying sexual relationship. In addition to specific sexual practices, spouses may also discover that they have different interests and inhibitions with respect to the timing and the context of sex. *Timing* would be whether a couple has sex at the end of the day, in the morning, or at mid-day; *location* means does sex only occur in the bedroom or are other venues sometimes used; and *environment* would include things such as using candles, wearing lingerie, or getting away to a hotel from time to time.

Healthy and Unhealthy Inhibitions

It is very important for couples to first figure out the true source of a spouse's reluctance to participate in a particular sexual behavior. In this examination, spouses need to distinguish between healthy inhibitions and unhealthy inhibitions. *Healthy inhibitions* are a spouse's authentic personal preferences, and correspond to his or her personal values about sexuality. Healthy inhibitions can be confirmed by otherwise positive attitudes about sex, and a desire to foster a proper amount of creativity in sexual expression; they are not based in anxiety or negative sexual conditioning about sex. Sometimes spouses simply do not enjoy certain types of sexual acts, or do not feel pleasure in the physical sensations created by some behaviors.

One spouse may also suggest sexual experimentation that does not align with the other spouse's values about what is "out of bounds" in marital sexuality. For example, foreplay that includes pornography, or initiating sex in a setting that may not be sufficiently private will go against many spouses' definition of sexual morality. Spouses need to find responsive and loving ways to work through differences based on healthy inhibitions. Attempts to get a spouse to "give in" by pouting, making him or her feel guilty, or by withdrawing love are always counter-productive; don't allow such things to get in the way of true intimacy and candid dialogue around these types of differences.

Other differences in sexual practices may be the by-product of *unhealthy inhibitions.* These types of inhibitions are often shaped by past experiences, outside perspectives, or negative sexual conditioning or trauma, rather than by authentic personal preferences or values. Spouses with unhealthy inhibitions tend to avoid creativity in sexual encounters, and are generally uncomfortable with their own sexual response—regardless of the specific forms of touch or stimulation. Both spouses would do well to remember that their partner's sexual practice desires are always more than mere physical actions; they symbolize their hopes for connection, excitement, and acceptance. They want to feel desirable; they want to feel masculine or feminine; they want to feel in love with each other. Spouses should cleave unto each other, and do their best to make unified decisions about what is appropriate for them as a couple. Decisions about what is "in-bounds" in marital sexuality should be made through personal lines of revelation and couple-only discussions, rather than through the priesthood line of revelation or by consulting with others (for more about this refer to Chapter 16).

Pace of Arousal

Another common difference between husbands and wives is the pace of arousal in their sexual response. As we noted in Chapter Nine, spouses rarely have matching thresholds for arousal and orgasm; this automatically creates a "faster" spouse and a "slower" spouse with respect to the pace of arousal and ease of orgasm.

For some couples, differences in their pace of arousal are small and inconsequential; but for others, the pace of arousal can be surprisingly disparate. For instance, some research suggests that for some couples, the wife's sexual arousal may take up to ten times longer than the husband's. This means that if the husband is able to reach full arousal and orgasm in two to three minutes, the wife may need 20 to 30 minutes to reach a comparable level of arousal and orgasm. This reminds us of the value of responsiveness and sufficient foreplay in sex in order to insure that intimacy is an enjoyable and fulfilling experience for both spouses.

You may recall our story of Jenny and Steve; Jenny felt exhausted by Steve's "high desire," and was considering not expressing any signs of affection for fear it might lead to something more. Jenny and Steve may benefit from candidly assessing each other's sexual desire differences. Steve enjoys sex and wants to have sex often; but he is not seeing Jenny's need for more emotional intimacy or non-arousing intimacy. Steve may begin to feel unwanted because Jenny is pulling back and withholding her affection. But if they were to acknowledge each other's sexual desire differences, they could then find ways to meet both the non-arousing desires of Jenny and the arousing/orgasmic desires of Steve. Maybe Steve could talk more about his emotions, as well as take more time to arouse Jenny so that she feels unhurried, fully engaged, and has a greater desire for arousal/orgasmic intimacy. Jenny should be able to voice her frustrations, and then openly look for creative ways to be sexual—either in non-arousing ways (by cuddling, flirting, or hugging), or in arousing ways. Such a paradigm shift could make the other's experience just as important as their own.

Ironically, a marriage comprised of a so-called "faster spouse" and a so-called "slower spouse" can create a beautiful balance for those who make unity a top priority. A quickly-aroused spouse usually initiates sex more frequently, thus helping them prioritize sex, and making sure that they regularly connect in sexual ways; and a slower-aroused spouse usually helps a couple appreciate the "journey of sex," by giving priority to the art of psychological and physical stimulation, thus creating more memorable and prolonged intimate encounters. In teaching this remarkable principle to young adults and couples, we sometimes tell them to make the "first rule of hiking" their "first rule of marital intimacy." The first rule of hiking is that they can only go as fast as the slowest hiker in their group—or else someone will get left behind. The same is true of arousing and orgasmic sex in marriage: couples should only go as fast as the "slowest" spouse—or else someone will get left behind! Learning to recognize and then respond to the pace of arousal during specific sexual experiences may be one of the best examples of unselfish love between spouses, as it helps couples create mutually satisfying sexual experiences.

Questions to Ponder:

1. *How do I deal with sexual desire differences?*

2. *When the pace of my sexual relationship is too fast—or too slow, how do I respond?*

3. *If differences and conflicts provide an opportunity for me to be truly responsive and selfless toward my spouse, how do I use these opportunities? How does my spouse handle such special opportunities?*

4. *Am I willing to experiment with new sexual practices?*

11

Different Pathways to Climax: Fostering Female Orgasm

In the last few chapters we have talked about physical differences between men and women and some of the more common sexual differences couples face. In this chapter we will address female orgasm and the conditions that create the best environment for wives to attain sexual satisfaction. It is very helpful for both spouses to understand the unique qualities of the female sexual experience. Over the years we have noticed that much of the information available about sex either talks about sex from only a male perspective, or it infers that sex is really the same for both men and women. The truth is, sex is a very gendered experience, where husbands and wives usually have divergent views about the sexual part of their marriage. So we believe that it is not only necessary to candidly talk about sex, but to also talk about sex from a female perspective. Additionally, we have noticed that too many couples struggle to make sex as appealing and pleasurable for the wife as it is for the husband. Even though husbands and wives do enjoy sex together, the route for becoming aroused and reaching climax is significantly different for each; the male pathway is quite simple and straightforward; but the female pathway tends to be more complex and multifaceted.

Even though this chapter is about female sexual response, it is not written for women only. In fact, this may be the most couple-oriented chapter in the whole book! Both spouses should carefully read, reread and discuss the vital concepts in this chapter. Your goal as spouses should be to learn about each other's bodies, minds, and emotions; such key knowledge will show you how to enjoy each other and deepen your relationship through sex. Sex is designed to unify; but to really unify, each spouse must thoroughly learn about and understand their partner. Once you sincerely accept the divine differences in male and female sexual arousal and desire, you will find that they can actually enhance your sexual relationship, making sex much more pleasurable for both of you.

To begin our discussion of fostering female orgasm, we would like to revisit two of the couples we introduced in the first chapter: Joshua's relationship and Jenny's relationship. Joshua was the husband who was attending a workshop on marriage enrichment and was surprised to learn that many women find it difficult to reach orgasm through intercourse alone. He also did not know that women usually take much longer than men to reach the orgasmic threshold. During a moment of difficult introspection, he faced the probability that he may have a problem with premature ejaculation, and that his wife had not been getting much out of their sexual relationship for many years—mostly because of his incorrect assumptions. It came as somewhat of a pointed revelation to him that he needs to care as much about what sex is like for her as it is for him. Likewise, his wife may not be prioritizing her own sexual needs by avoiding talking to him about ways she feels their relationship can improve.

Jenny's challenge is not physical in nature because her husband, Steve, understands the physical parts of sexual arousal and they have had mutually orgasmic sexual experiences. Jenny's main concern is that her husband is almost exclusively focusing on the physical parts of their relationship, and that sex is just about the only thing he has much interest in doing together. This leaves Jenny feeling more used than loved. Steve is so interested in sex and finds it so enjoyable that he just assumes that Jenny must feel the same way. When their relationship began to decline, he naively assumed the solution was to try some new techniques or sexual positions. And recently, Jenny is finding sex aversive and is starting to avoid both physical contact and emotional disclosure with Steve. To begin to genuinely repair their marriage, Steve needs to learn how to see their relationship through Jenny's eyes, and acknowledge that sex fits into their relationship differently for her than it does for him. Also, Jenny needs to be aware of how her lack of authenticity and disclosure with Steve is robbing him of the opportunity to hear and respond to her concerns.

Divinely Determined Differences

Sometimes when couples hear the statistics that wives often take four times longer to reach orgasm, need ten times the stimulation to become aroused, or may not achieve orgasm through intercourse alone, they conclude that women must be "the problem" when it comes to sex in marriage. Nothing could be further from the truth. In our quest for sexual wholeness in marriage, ironically, seeing things from the wife's perspective is often the solution rather than the problem. As we described in Chapter 10, differences in sexual desire and arousal are rather common in most couples. Differences aside, however, one problem in Joshua's relationship is that neither of the spouses have made her experience as important as his experience—so they both have been missing out on the joy of mutually satisfying sexual experiences. But this is a solvable predicament.

Additionally, we may think that men are more sexual than women, but there is strong evidence that women are just as sexual—if not more so—than men. We know that biologically, wives are created to feel sexual enjoyment and orgasm as consistently and as frequently as their husbands. And further, because women do not have a refractory period like men, women have the potential to have multiple orgasms during one sexual encounter. Nevertheless, a compensating factor is that fostering orgasm for women is a more complex process than it is for men—for which we should be very grateful! Physiologically speaking, a husband's sexual response is quite straightforward: stimulate a man's penis and generally he will reach orgasm rather quickly, but wives are typically much more complex and simply do not work this way.

Responsiveness to Her Preferences

Physical stimulation should meet a woman's needs. Like their husbands, wives have certain areas of their bodies that when touched can stimulate desire and arousal. But, unlike men, direct and repetitive stimulation of the genitals is typically not sufficient to create full arousal. In fact, if that is the only type of stimulation, it may actually irritate more than it stimulates. Husbands should deliberately listen to their partners' wants and let that guide their foreplay. This is probably where Joshua needs the most growth. If they were to reshape their sexual relationship by having his wife lead, it would open up an entirely new world of sexual enjoyment that both have so far missed out on. Granted, this shift may be as difficult for her as it is for Joshua, since it has been easier to just have him take the lead, yet it has not been as fulfilling for her.

To cultivate arousal and orgasm for wives, the purpose of the clitoris can hardly be overemphasized. As we noted in Chapter Seven, the clitoris is a very small part of a woman's anatomy that has no other function other than to provide sexual arousal. Specifically, the concentrated nerves of the clitoris extend in a wishbone-like shape underneath both sides of the outer and inner labia, which makes areas in the genital region more or less arousing. Almost this entire area arouses a woman, and is open to deft stimulation that may be less obvious than the direct target of the clitoris. Because each woman has their own unique pattern of nerve clusters in the pelvic region, it is impossible for us to describe—or for any husband to innately know—what may feel best at a particular time in a particular sexual encounter. It is crucial, therefore, for wives to show their husbands how to skillfully touch these areas, and to find certain positions that create enough contact to produce stimulation that will help activate lubrication and arousal.

As women become aroused, their vaginal walls secrete small drops of lubricant that helps to avoid otherwise painful penetration. Foreplay that causes a woman to lubricate is usually a good indicator that the touch is appropriate and arousing. However, a woman's sexual arousal pattern should not be reduced to a mere question of whether she is lubricating. Jenny's body is responsive to Steve's touch, but she still does not usually find sexual fulfillment because of the other areas in their relationship that are lacking. Therefore, we should talk about desire and arousal as they fit in the bigger picture of a relationship; this should help spouses understand each other's pattern of arousal much more than just focusing on physical indicators.

If a wife is not allowed to reach her arousal and orgasm thresholds because of a husband's impatience or his lack of understanding, sex can become drudgery rather than a pleasant experience. If this is the case, she can play a key role by helping her husband to learn about her body. She can guide him to where, how, and when he should touch her. If a particular movement or touch becomes irritating after it is repeated a number of times, she can guide him to a different area of her body, or suggest a new type of touch or movement. If wives will provide this specific guidance and husbands will welcome it, the couple can make quick progress in learning how to satisfy each other. Each can act as a "gentle teacher" and "willing student" during sexual discovery. The goal is to complement one another, look to each other's needs, and enjoy the pleasure of physically being together.

Arousing Her Heart

Even though wives respond to physical stimulation that is artfully done, so much more goes into their full equation of sexual arousal. How emotionally close she perceives the relationship to be, and the nature of the couple's daily conversations, are critical components of her sexual interest. Additionally, a couple's tenderness, openness, and shared vulnerability may often be more arousing to a woman than physical touch. Whether or not her husband understands her emotions and is responsive to her needs can enhance or diminish her erotic desires. Women want to belong, but if they are rushed through the sexual process, they may conclude that their partner is unavailable for their own sexual needs. And this can bring poignant feelings of loneliness and sadness. But when sexual experiences have an atmosphere of compassion and mutual appreciation, both spouses can revel amid priceless feelings of security and stability.

Both physical and psychological stimulation is generally necessary for women to become aroused. This is the central problem in Jenny and Steve's relationship, where psychological stimulation is almost entirely absent. Neither one has been willing to admit or prioritize their bigger emotional needs, which has left only Steve's sexual desires to drive their expressions of love since early courtship. Most women, like Jenny, are especially in tune with psychological stimulation, and may put up barriers that thwart physical stimulation if they feel a dearth of emotional sensitivity by their husbands. So giving a good deal of attention to both physical and psychological stimulation is vital for women.

Striving for Sexual Balance

As discussed in Chapter 10, pacing is a primary factor of the sexual experience. Even though men can usually reach orgasm quickly and consistently, speed is not always the most useful approach—particularly if couples value a deeper emotional connection during sex. The divinely shaped differences in the partnership of sex prompts husbands to slow down, try new approaches, and they will soon find that this adds so much to their wife's pleasure. A slower pace is about time, and time communicates attentiveness, priority, and a desire to truly be with each other. Slowing down the process is an astounding benefit to women—and therefore to men as well. Allowing enough time for the woman to reach her orgasm threshold may require a couple to engage in more emotional sharing and unhurried affectionate touch; the wife's need for these adds more depth to the physical component of sex.

Likewise, the higher frequency of sex that many husbands desire can help wives learn the value of initiating and prioritizing this key facet of their relationship. You can see how each of these differences complement the other, and combine to bring balance to the broader sexual experience. Even though men may respond quickly, without the balance of a partner who slows the process down, much of the meaning of sex may be lost. It takes time for the richness of the encounter to impact a couple. So if men are always in control of the tempo and agenda of sex, much may be missed. The balance of men's sexual consistency, mixed with the complexity of women's need for variety and emotional depth, can make for a very enriching sexual life. Women respond better when the sexual experience is part emotional, part spiritual, and part physical. A woman can encourage her husband in the emotional dimension by making eye contact during sex, by describing her current emotions about sexuality, and by urging him to do the same. We find that when women add their actual voices to sex, the level of unity and couple satisfaction increases.

If men are conscientious to the special female dimensions of sexuality, sex can become much more than mere physical pleasure. Unifying sex completes a relationship in a spiritual, emotional, and physical way; couples can feel more balanced in every area of their lives. But to achieve this balance, the couple must pay more careful attention to the sexual enjoyment of the wife, which is too often overlooked.

Problems That Women Face

One issue that impedes arousal and orgasm is when a woman is worried about other factors during sex: how she looks, her performance, how the children are doing in school, whether sex will result in pregnancy, and so on. Women should remind themselves that Heavenly Father instituted sex for reproduction and more; it is meant to be fun, playful, strengthen bonds, and express love. If women will relax, let go of other concerns, and allow themselves to be fully in the present moment, it can help build sexual desire and arousal, and move a woman closer to orgasm. Likewise, if women are always outward focused (serving others, concern for children, etc.), they will miss the intricate introspection that is essential to reach orgasm.

Women would do well to believe that their sexual needs are as important as their partner's. A woman can show this by taking time to learn about her own body, finding out what touch, movement, intensity, duration, or other activities arouse her; and then she can teach her husband how to satisfy her sexually. Some discoveries may occur during foreplay or intercourse. Understanding and embracing these nuances promotes an easier arousal in women, and is fundamental to a good sexual relationship. It can be a great thrill to explore with each other which types of touch, movement, intensity, position, or activity can bring sexual felicity.

One common impediment to embracing this idea of differences is because we are used to men being the sexual initiators and directors; changing this may feel inappropriate—or even wrong—to some couples. Some ask, *Aren't men supposed to be more interested and capable in this area? Shouldn't the man take the lead?* It is indeed lamentable if couples do not challenge such dysfunctional beliefs, and learn to enjoy sexual encounters that are directed by the wife. Especially since her sexual response is more complicated, male initiated and male directed sexual encounters may be the primary obstacle to mutual satisfaction.

When a woman successfully focuses her thoughts on her own arousal, she may be surprised to find out that her husband gets enormous satisfaction from seeing her experience orgasm. And once a woman sees the dual pleasures brought on by her arousal, it is easier for her to let her husband watch her, with an *I-am-so-happy-for-you!* smile on his face. A woman can invite her husband to enjoy her body as she enjoys his. When men and women promote sexual preparation and play with the woman in mind, they are adhering to one of the Lord's purposes for giving sex to married couples:

> *Sexual relations within marriage are divinely approved not only for the purpose of procreation, but also a means of expressing love and strengthening emotional and spiritual ties between husband and wife* (*www.lds.org*, Gospel Topics: Birth Control).

Developing Healthy Attitudes

Some people were raised in an environment where sex was not discussed openly or appropriately. In these cases, inaccurate or unhelpful attitudes about sex are naturally carried into the marriage. Many of these attitudes originate from the common yet mistaken belief that the Church prohibits certain sexual behaviors or forms of sexual exploration. For example, some believe that intercourse is the only acceptable approach to sexual enjoyment; or that spouses should never touch their own bodies; or that they should not in any way contribute to their own arousal during sex. Such misconceptions limit wholesome and healthy sexual exploration. This type of thinking is especially detrimental to women because they require more foreplay, stimulation, and time to fully arouse. Varied kinds of foreplay and sexual experimentation are essential for meeting wives' needs, since the stimulation created during intercourse is generally not enough for them to reach orgasm. Spouses should adopt healthy and sound attitudes about sex that gives them liberty to discover the divine sexual potential of each other's bodies, and infuse excitement and bonding into a relationship that is designed to last forever.

If a couple maturely reflects on these types of limiting attitudes, and honestly questions why they hold to certain views, only then should they make decisions together about what best works in their own relationship. They may be surprised to discover that a wife who teaches her husband how to arouse her by letting him watch her arouse herself, can be a healthy part of building a relationship. Or she may want to coach him during foreplay or intercourse to understand what movement, position, or pressure is most stimulating. If the intent of sexual activities are to build a relationship, to teach, or to please each other, they are not selfish; they strength the bonds of marriage.

Exploring different sexual positions can add some needed variety, and can also increase stimulation to particular areas of a woman's body. Discovering which positions work best for your situation can be an enjoyable adventure, as long as you both can be lighthearted about it. Many women may find that they have more control of the force and speed of movement if they are on top. Other women may feel better stimulation from deeper penetration and prefer sitting positions. The typical position of the man on top is often a favorite because many couples get the best results from this position; yet even with this position, it may be helpful to experiment with different nuances such as raising or bending the women's legs at different angles to find more enjoyment.

Many LDS couples have found that oral sex is useful in bringing the wife to orgasm. Compared to hand stimulation, the reduced pressure and lower friction of oral stimulation is more effective for many women. Other couples have chosen to not engage in oral sex, but instead use personal lubricant products that help the wife feel stimulation without irritating friction. We encourage couples to discuss these matters candidly, and make mature decisions for their own relationship as to what is helpful, appropriate, and enjoyable. In making these decisions, carefully consider the following four important questions:

1. Does this particular behavior strengthen our relationship with each other and with God?

2. Do we both agree about this aspect of our sexuality?

3. Does this reflect a positive and healthy attitude about sexuality?

4. Does this nurture the sexual needs of my spouse and myself?

These questions should not be answered by simply labeling certain behaviors as "right" or "wrong;" rather, you should thoughtfully consider the motives and consequences of proposed sexual behaviors. We discuss this important decision making process in more detail in Chapter 16.

Concluding Thoughts

Let's return to the two couples mentioned at the beginning of this chapter. How can they improve their situations? Both couples can have an entirely new sexual experience if they give first priority to the woman's needs and preferences for a while. This does not mean that the male's needs will be neglected or always be in the background; it simply means that to overcome the misconstrued idea that sex should be a male-directed activity, it is crucial for them to see what it's like to have the wives in the driver's seat for a season. It should yield very good fruit.

Jenny should educate Steve, and insist that the larger emotional and psychological needs of their relationship are attended to with regularity. She should reject the idea that acting like her husband would be the best solution to their problems. Steve will need to control his sexual impulses and learn to be emotionally and psychologically attentive; it may be a difficult transition. It may even be necessary to have a redo of their courtship, where for a few weeks or months they practice courting skills such as talking, sharing, and enjoying activities that are not centered on sex. While strict abstinence during this time may not be necessary, Steve should make some sacrifices that will mean a great deal; he should let Jenny dictate the when, what, and how often of their sexual relationship for a while. Implementing these suggestions will probably work wonders, especially if her husband does not sulk if he thinks that his sexual needs are being put on the back burner.

Joshua's path to an improved sexual relationship will probably be quite different than Jenny's. Because Joshua has realized on his own that he has not been very attentive to his wife, he can more easily approach her and initiate a change. What may be harder for them to figure out is why, for all these years, she did not speak up and assert her needs. If she has a passive personality, it will make it harder for her to take the lead, or even to acknowledge that she has any sexual preferences. Both couples will need a good measure of maturity to candidly discuss ways to develop a more balanced sexual relationship; it will be a challenge and could take some time to get it right. But it is a challenge worth pursuing; it is unrealistic to expect an easy and simple transition from a more one-sided sexual relationship to a mutually satisfying one.

As couples take courage and address the issues of a woman's orgasm, they will inevitably learn more about each other and thereby strengthen their relationship. They should enjoy this journey and experiment until they have found several ways that are mutually enjoyable and likely to result in both partners reaching orgasm. Couples will see the beauty of expanded sexual encounters that last longer, include more teasing, more play, more variety, and more enjoyment because of the special opportunities that are inherent in gender differences. As we have learned, such gender differences are designed to complement each other, and add a facet to the relationship that brings an opportunity for personal growth and a deeper understanding of one another. One of the priceless blessings of being members of the Church is our conviction that we can learn what we need to learn by the influence of the Gift of the Holy Ghost. The Spirit can literally teach us things we had never considered; it can also help us distinguish truth from myth; the Spirit can help us align our sexual paradigm to eternal truths; and it can help us see what our spouses need most.

Questions to Ponder:

1. *What are the differences of arousal and climax for women?*

2. *What is the purpose of the clitoris and how it is stimulated?*

3. *How do I show that I value the special dimension women bring to the sexual experience?*

4. *Am I holding on to any attitudes that may inhibit my ability to communicate my needs, listen to my spouse's needs, or that severely limit sexual activity?*

5. *Is sex mutually enjoyable? Does it tend to favor one partner?*

6. *Am I open to creativity in sex? Am I passive, or do I initiate creativity?*

12

THE EMOTIONAL DIMENSION: SEXUAL COMMUNICATION

As we consider the four couples introduced in Chapter One, there is the potential that their sexual differences may create disappointment, conflict, and even contention. However, if couples accept the idea that their sexual responses are designed to complement each other, they are much more likely to respect— even cherish—these differences. This is the goal of the emotional dimension of sexual wholeness. Sexually mature spouses express love in ways that build the relationship and add to the foundation of positive sexual symbolism. Such expressions of love are measured by the *quality of the communication* between spouses and their ability to *manage differences and conflict*. By looking at these patterns of communication, we can determine a couple's commitment to the process of intimacy, and see how they engage in both validation and confrontation in their relationship.

Sexual wholeness requires kind and candid communication about the sexual relationship—both during as well as in-between sexual encounters. Sex always conveys unspoken symbols and unspoken messages, but couples need to engage in spoken and direct communication if they want to build shared meanings of their sex life. In this chapter, we discuss specific facets of how couples communicate, and how they become a key part of spouses' sense of sexual wholeness.

Communication During Sex

As we mentioned previously, optimal physical stimulation and satisfying sexual experiences can be achieved only if spouses are willing to make their body sensations and sexual desires known to each other during sex. This is very sensitive communication, where spouses share the most private parts of themselves with one another. How well couples communicate during their sexual encounters determines whether they stay in synch with each other, as well as how much trust and security is fostered between them.

It is important to note that effective communication during sex should have a proper harmony between non-verbal and verbal messages, and requires spouses to be authentic and open. Many of the messages spouses need to share during sex are non-verbal. Spontaneously expressing—rather than repressing—our sexual responses is an endearing form of communication. Both men and women are endowed with an innate magnetism to certain sexual cues, such as the human form and the arousal process of the opposite sex. So when spouses see, hear, and feel their spouse's sexual responses—such as changes in breathing patterns, skin flushing, moaning, and other physical reactions to sexual stimulation—they usually become highly aroused themselves. If they allow themselves to become "lost in the moment," and not become self-conscious or hold back their sexual responses, they will be giving authentic non-verbal cues of what they find sexually pleasing. Other helpful forms of non-verbal communication include placing a spouse's hands where you would like them, or moving yourself into a desirable position.

Verbal communication during sex is sometimes the best way for spouses to share what they are experiencing. This may be as simple as saying that a certain type of touch feels good, or giving progressive instructions to enhance the arousal process. At times, verbal communication during sex may include suggesting a new form of sexuality. Expressing such inner desires is a vulnerable process that tests the level of responsiveness in the relationship. However, if spouses are responsive and validating in these instances, they can become increasingly comfortable with creativity and openness in their sexuality. Too many couples avoid the risk and shy away from this vulnerability, and instead, just assume that their spouse knows what they want.

Initiating sexual contact is a particularly vulnerable form of sexual communication. As a partner puts himself or herself "out there" by either verbally or non-verbally requesting sex, there is a risk of rejection. This process is what marriage experts call *making a bid*. Relationship *bids* include verbal or non-verbal requests for attention, interaction, or affection. Specific sexual bids create a precarious moment where the answer is either responsive (e.g., acceptance, validation, awareness, etc.) or non-responsive (e.g., rejection, minimizing, devaluing, etc.).

There are three ways that spouses can respond to relationship bids, including sexual bids: turning toward, turning away, and turning against. *Turning toward* your spouse does not require that every bid for sexual initiation actually leads to sex. There will be legitimate times in every marriage when a sexual bid can legitimately be turned down. Even on these few occasions, spouses can still turn toward each other by clearly sending a message of "Not now, but I'd enjoy it later;" this conveys a dramatically different message than just saying "No." *Turning away* from one's spouse is when spouses give no response at all, or play down the initiation bid. *Turning against* one's spouse includes making them feel embarrassed or shamed over their bid for sexual contact; if these types of responses become a pattern, spouses may become very reluctant to bid or disclose their desires. This can lead to intense sexual frustration and embittered conflict, and inhibit most sexual desire and arousal patterns in the relationship.

Communication About Sex

Even with effective communication during sex, nearly all couples will find times when their relationship can benefit from more extensive conversations about their sexual habits. This is particularly true if spouses are feeling out of synch with each other. There are times in nearly all marriages when the sexual tides are in and when the sexual tides are out, so to speak. Sexual communication can also include coy messages that convey sexual interest, attraction, and anticipation. These flirtatious and fun communiques create a private, ongoing dialogue between spouses that invigorates their relationship.

Above all, marriage research stresses the need for couples to pay attention to their communication patterns, and to be willing to work at improving authentic and healthy communication skills. At its roots, effective sexual communication is how well spouses listen to each other—with their hearts as well as their ears—and openly divulge their sexual needs and desires. Over time, a couple's relationship will either be strengthened through the presence of—or eroded by the absence of—effective sexual communication. Such patient listening can cultivate true intimacy, heal hurts, and strengthen the sense of partnership. When you communicate in this way, your spouse is much more likely to trust you, thus opening the door for ongoing intimate communications and more positive sexual interactions.

Empathetic Listening

Empathetic listening is the art of connecting with another person in a way that they feel like you fully understand what they are saying and feeling. The goal of empathetic listening is to help another person feel not only understood but valued. It is a vital skill in marriage generally, and is a critical part of expressing sexual love specifically. How *well* you listen largely depends upon *how* you listen. To be an effective listener, your spouse must first believe that you really *want* to listen. They must feel that when they tell you something, you really care about what they are saying.

Effective listening must be based on a foundation of mature love. If you do not really care about what your spouse is saying, there is no clever technique you can use to convince him or her that you do. You may get away with "pretending to care" from time to time, but in the long run he or she will always discover the true intents of your heart. Effective listeners learn to listen beyond the words that are spoken. Empathetic listeners let you know that they want to hear what you have to say. This is especially needed when spouses are trying to share their sexual selves. The disclosure of deep sexual desires—as well as discomforts or inhibitions— makes a spouse very vulnerable. The only way spouses may feel safe enough to share their inner sexual desires is if there has been a habit of loving and attentive listening. Here are some suggestions for making sure that as a listener, you understand the messages your spouse is trying to share with you. How well you do these things is a good indicator of how loving of a spouse you are, and whether you are inviting intimate disclosure—or shutting such disclosure down.

1. Listen More Than You Talk

You cannot listen while you are talking. Don't be thinking about what you are going to say next; give your full attention to what your spouse is trying to say.

2. Pay Attention to Nonverbal Language:

Physical gestures, facial expressions, tone of voice, and body posture are parts of any communication, and are often the most important part of sexual messages. Communication experts have found that only seven percent of a message's meaning is conveyed by spoken words; 38 percent of that is portrayed by tone of voice. Nearly 55 percent of a message's meaning is conveyed without words.

3. Listen For What is *Not* Said

Ask questions to clarify the meaning of certain words used, or ask your spouse to share more thoughts and feelings. Some find it very difficult to speak up about matters that are highly emotional for them, such as sex. Listen for how your spouse presents the message. What he or she hesitates to say is often the most critical point of the message.

4. Determine Exactly What the Other Person is Saying

Reflect back to your spouse what you think they have said, in a "shared meaning" experience. Fully understand the meaning and content of their message before you try to reply to it. A good listener does not assume understanding; he or she has it confirmed.

5. Manage Your Emotions

Don't let your emotions interfere with your listening. If spouses feel like they are being confronted, they will begin to feel exposed, hurt, embarrassed, or devalued. Additionally, if emotions get out of hand, there is a tendency to become defensive, pout, and withdraw from sharing their differing inner experience. You don't have to agree to be a good listener. Don't argue: even if you win, you both lose.

6. Empathize With Your Spouse

Try to "walk in the other person's shoes" so that you can understand things from their perspective. Differences in sexual desire and preferences are normal and should be expected in marriage; you have different bodies and are different people. But these very differences are what can make sexual connection so meaningful and rewarding.

Clear-Sending Communication

In addition to empathetic listening, loving sexual communication needs to include clearly sent messages between spouses. This is the "talking part" of sexual communication. Ironically, most unclear communications about sex in marriage have nothing to do with actual difficulties in forming words. Sexual messages become unclear when background issues cause people to not be direct, open, and authentic in their statements. Consider why Jenny is reluctant to talk directly to Steve about her growing resistance to be sexual with him. Such lack of directness is often a sign that one or both spouses is struggling with emotional insecurity, and a lack of belonging in the relationship. As we discussed in Chapter Five, nearly all couples grapple with the intimacy of validation and the intimacy of confrontation. Yet both types provide the only way couples can balance and integrate their needs for belonging and becoming. So for these types of intimacy to flourish in a marriage, we have to be an authentic and loving spouse.

For clear-sending sexual communication, spouses need to be authentic; they should *"say what they mean and mean, what they say"*—all with great respect as equals. Sound relationships are built on the communication of the truth. If spouses won't frankly state their true thoughts or feelings, trust and closeness are restrained. If the purpose of our communication is to disapprove, manipulate, cover up, deceive, threaten, hurt, or make someone feel guilty, we are far from being authentic. Furthermore, if spouses let their emotions or personal insecurities dictate what they say, they will send less authentic messages. However, if each one tries to use clear-sending communication—combined with empathetic listening, these skills will help them effectively express love and concern for one another in ways where they will both feel understood.

Recall Joshua and his wife; Joshua was unaware that his wife needed more stimulation until learning about it in class. Despite his wife's infrequent orgasms, Joshua assumed she was still satisfied. This situation is an example of the communication issues we are discussing. So if Joshua's wife clearly communicates her needs, and if Joshua is empathic in his response, such sexual satisfaction issues can be openly discussed in a kind, vulnerable way.

Meta-Communication

One of the more important types of clear-sending communication a couple should use in their sexual relationship is called *meta-communication*, or talking about communication. For example, if partners sit down to talk about what happened in the argument they just had, they are meta-communicating. With respect to sexual intimacy, when spouses talk about sex and their sexual encounters with each other, they are using meta-communication. This type of "relationship talk" is a key part of any mature relationship. In fact, regular and constructive meta-communication is one of the chief skills that couples should develop before they become engaged or married.

Managing Sexual Conflict

As couples try to deal with their differences, sometimes poor communication habits—and a lack of responsiveness—can bring on feelings of frustration, anger, and sadness. Of course it would be ideal if all couples always handled their differences in supportive and mature ways, but in reality, most couples handle differences poorly at times. Once we properly understand differences in marriage, we may find that openly dealing with those differences—and even having occasional disagreements about sex—can be a sign of a healthy marriage. Most of us express our frustrations only if we feel safe, and expect our thoughts to be carefully considered. We should strive to become mature partners who feel comfortable enough to share their opinions, preferences—and frustrations.

For both happy and unhappy couples, the pattern of conflict starts with *differences*, and then *complaints*. Up until the point of *conflict,* the general pathway is the same for all couples. At the point of conflict, however, there is a critical crossroad where some couples manage their conflict well—and increase their intimacy, while other couples manage their conflict poorly—and engage in contention. The Lord taught, "he that hath the spirit of contention is not of me, but is of the devil, who is the father of contention" (3 Nephi 11:29). There are some key factors that set the stage for either success or failure in the early stages of managing sexual conflict. Let's examine each of these factors.

Complaints: Start-up and Accepting Influence

Researchers such as Dr. John Gottman have found that 96 percent of the time, the way a discussion begins is the way it will end. So if a spouse begins a discussion of sexual differences using a *harsh startup*—such as being negative, accusatory, or using criticism—the discussion is destined to fail. On the other hand, if that same spouse begins the discussion using a *softened startup*, the discussion will most likely end on the same positive tone. Now, this principle is particularly important for women to pay attention to because research shows that women bring up issues 80 percent of the time in couple relationships! When it comes to sexual complaints, however, the pattern is not so lopsided, so men better pay attention too! Your choice of using either a harsh or a softened startup sets the stage to how responsive your partner will be to your complaint. Research shows that if their partner softens their startup during conflict, spouses are significantly more responsive to the conversation; it follows that harsh startups increase the chance that your message will be rejected.

Another important part of the complaint process is how responsive or accepting spouses are of the message. The stage is set for a positive conversation when a spouse accepts influence and respectfully listens to the complaint, rather than "batting it back" at their partner. Now, this principle is particularly important for men to pay attention to, because if research shows that women *bring up* complaints 80 percent of the time, this means that men will be the *receiver* of these messages 80 percent of the time! Again, this pattern may not be as lopsided when it comes to *sexual* complaints, so women will also be on the receiving end of complaints. Researchers have also discovered that how spouses *accept influence* (or, how much they are open to being influenced by the other), is a major predictor of whether a relationship will last. Spouses can fail to accept influence from each other by disengaging from the conversation, or by minimizing the issue, or in more hostile ways such as becoming contentious and belligerent. Sound relationships are characterized by *dialogue*—rather than *gridlock*—with issues of conflict.

Learn How to Handle Differences Constructively

There are three simple questions couples can ask themselves to determine whether they are handling differences constructively; these are skill based, and skills can be acquired.

1. When discussing differences, do we stay focused on resolving the issue?

Often when couples discuss specific sexual differences, they begin to argue, or their conversations veer off into other topics and complaints. Once the focus of the discussion has faded, discussing issues is more likely to hurt your relationship than bring you together. Couples should set a pattern of discussing differences in ways that focus on compromise and finding solutions—not on winning arguments.

2. Do we control our emotions during conflict?

If spouses allow themselves to become flooded with emotions during discussions, they are rarely able to address their differences in a positive way. *Emotional flooding* usually triggers physiological changes such as an increased heart rate, the secretion of adrenalin, and an increase in blood pressure. Such physiological changes make it almost impossible for partners to maintain a positive discussion. And once you are emotionally flooded, your brain's capacity to process information is reduced, meaning it's harder to pay attention to what your partner is saying. A problem solving discussion where one or both partners become flooded is doomed to fail; the issue should be tabled and revisited later. The cure for flooding is softened startup and soothing. Partners need to learn to bring up concerns about their sexual relationship in non-blaming ways, and find ways to soothe themselves and each other during discussions so that negative emotions stay in check.

3. Do we maintain respect and concern for one another during an argument?

Marriage scholars have found that in successful marriages, spouses maintain high levels of respect and mutual regard for one another—even during an argument. Sometimes spouses allow arguments to degrade into episodes of criticism and personal attacks. This can have lasting detrimental effects on couple unity, causing some spouses to emotionally withdraw from the relationship. Maintaining respect for one another sends the message that your relationship is more important than the problems you are currently facing, and that you are on the same side in trying to find constructive ways to deal with your differences.

Positive Communication

Finally, we want to point out that how couples manage conflict is directly related to their level of friendship and positive communication. In his research, Dr. Gottman has identified the relationship skills that help couples manage conflict well. According to Dr. Gottman, these skills are based upon "gentleness" in conversation. In addition to using softened startup and accepting influence from one another, successful couples maintain at least a *5-to-1 ratio of positive-to-negative interactions* during conflict interactions. During such discussions, the ratio of positive to negative interactions in relationships headed for divorce is 0.8-to-1 — not 5-to-1 as it is in stable and happy couples. This accentuates the fact that the presence of positive emotions in a couple's relationship is crucial. Couples who make time to have fun together, and share in other enjoyable activities, foster an environment where they can then manage the inevitable conflicts that will come to nearly every marriage.

Questions to Ponder:

1. *Is it clear to my spouse that I understand what she/he is saying and feeling? Does this happen consistently?*

2. *Is it difficult for me to be candid and clear when I talk about sexual issues? If so, what is the source of my discomfort?*

3. *Do my spouse and I both participate in "relationship talk," or is our conversation usually one-sided?*

4. *Am I really trying to solve problems, or do I tend to blame people?*

5. *Am I more likely to start conversations harshly or with a soft startup?*

6. *Do I accept influence from my spouse?*

13

THE EMOTIONAL DIMENSION: EMOTIONAL SECURITY

Let us return to Shannon from the first chapter. You may recall that she was the one who learned about attachment styles, and determined that she had an anxious style. She rarely felt worthy of other people's love and support and was frequently seeking reassurance from those around her. Unfortunately, she found out that her husband had visited a pornographic website, and this again triggered insecurities about herself and her relationships. Even though many people would be distressed if they found out that their spouse was viewing pornographic media, Shannon's insecurities made a difficult situation even more challenging. For a person who has an anxious attachment style, it is common for other people's problems to be interpreted as a reflection of their own lack of "lovability." So Shannon not only has to figure out how to deal with her disappointment and feelings of betrayal because of her husband's behavior, she also feels responsible for his decisions, and thinks that his behavior is a reflection on how she isn't a good enough wife.

What makes Shannon's challenges even more difficult is the fact that her husband, David, has an avoidant attachment style. It is not uncommon for an anxious person to become attracted to an avoidant person, as the avoidant person's perceived strength and independence are seen as a good complement for their own insecurities. Unfortunately, avoidant people are usually not very good at helping anxious people feel more secure in their relationships, because avoidant partners usually avoid the relationship needs of others and try to remain aloof.

Attachment Styles and Sexuality

What are these attachment styles and how do they relate to sexuality? Even though we drew on principles of the Gospel when we talked about the need for belonging in previous chapters, the human need for emotional bonding is not unique to the restored Gospel of Jesus Christ. Similar concepts can be found in the social sciences that describe this basic human need to feel loved and be connected to others. For example, attachment theory, a highly regarded theory in developmental psychology, discusses the universal human need to develop secure attachments in loving and lasting relationships. According to attachment theory, all people have an innate psychological and biological system called the *attachment system*. This is a non-rational, innate system that motivates children to be close to their parents and loved ones—particularly in times of distress or danger.

In romantic relationships, attachment theory defines *attachment security* as feelings of confidence, safety, and security in the knowledge that one's partner will be available when desired or needed. Attachment scholars use the word *available* to describe emotional accessibility and physical responsiveness between spouses. In addition to accessibility and responsiveness, scholars have also found that open communication is a critical component of stable and secure attachment.

By contrast, threats to accessibility, responsiveness, and open communication can create *attachment insecurity* for both children and adults. Thus, when long-standing availability is lacking in a couple's relationship, attachment insecurity is the common result, which usually includes anxiety, avoidance, or both. When spouses are loving, warm, and responsive to one another, each spouse develops a sense that he or she is a person of value, one who is worthy of nurturing and sacrifice; they also sense that his or her partner is trustworthy and committed to the relationship. Dr. John Bowlby, the initial developer of attachment theory, explained it in this way:

> *Human beings of all ages are happiest and able to deploy their talents to best advantage when they are confident that, standing behind them, there are one or more trusted persons who will come to their aid should difficulties arise* (John Bowlby, 1979, The Making and Breaking of Affectional Bonds, *pp. 103-104).*

We learn in our early years whether we are valued and loved and we can count on people to help us through our difficulties. Those who have consistently loving caregivers develop a secure attachment style, whereas those who don't develop an insecure style that brings anxiety or avoidance. Those who are anxious express their insecurity by frequently seeking reassurance from others; anxious partners never seem to feel safe in their relationships, and thus seem suffocating to those with a secure style.

An avoidant person has learned to deal with their insecurities by becoming fiercely independent and aloof. Similar to anxious people, they have been conditioned to believe that others can't be fully trusted to be there when they need them; instead of seeking their approval and love, they do the opposite, and appear to not need much from others. But they are still every bit as lonely and insecure as anxious people; they just express it differently by not allowing others into their emotional life to avoid being hurt again.

There are those who may believe that bad childhood experiences somehow doom a person to a life of dysfunctional relationships. What they may not understand is that attachment is a never-ending process, so even though early childhood experiences do exert outsized effects on us as we become adults, new and healthy relationships can help people heal from previous bad relationships. So with respect to sexuality, each person should consider whether their attachment styles help or hinder their goals for a satisfying and reliable sexual relationship. Remember also that those who were raised with a secure attachment style can still become insecure after wading through a few difficult relationships with romantic partners.

What we do know about both adults and children is that if they feel more secure in their relationships, they are then able to take risks more in creatively addressing their own needs and those of their partners. Creativity and risk are two crucial components of sexuality that help couples not only avoid sexual monotony, but it leaves the door open where they can discuss their sexual relationship and address new challenges over the years. A secure attachment style helps individuals in countless ways in developing a mature approach to relationships and sexuality. So how does one know if they have a secure, anxious, or avoidant attachment style? Thoughtfully consider the questions in Table 13.1 to help evaluate yourself.

Table 13.1 — *What is My Personal Attachment Style?*

1. Do I find it difficult or awkward to get close to others?

2. Do I not trust most people?

3. Do people in my family or romantic relationships sometimes complain that I seem aloof or distant?

4. Do I generally feel that it is best just to depend on myself, and not rely on others?

5. Are other people reluctant to get as close to me as I would prefer?

6. Do I often worry that my romantic partners don't love me, or will leave me?

7. Do I sometimes get so close to others that they feel overwhelmed trying to meet my needs?

8. Do I usually feel anxious about how my relationship is going?

If you answered *yes* to any of questions 1,2 3 or 4, you may be leaning toward an avoidant attachment style. If you answered *yes* to any of questions 5, 6, 7 or 8, you may be leaning toward an anxious attachment style. If you did not answer *yes* to any of the questions, you may very well have a secure attachment style. If you are interested in pursuing a more thorough evaluation of your attachment styles and general relationship strengths, visit *https://www.relate-institute.org*. There are many sites that claim to quickly assess your relationships, but few are as scientifically valid and reliable as the "RELATE" and "READY" instruments found on this website.

Let's revisit Shannon and David's relationship to see how their attachment styles make their sexual challenges even more difficult. Shannon has an anxious attachment style and rarely feels that she is lovable. She usually thinks that she is undesirable both sexually and in other ways, so she is prone to depression and anxiety. Consequently, she finds it difficult to take care of herself and be consistent in her responsibilities. The extra weight she has put on, along with challenges keeping up with home, children, and church duties, add to her sense of not being a very good person. She seeks frequent reassurance from others—especially David; yet when others give her compliments, she usually discounts them or feels that people aren't telling her the truth.

David, on the other hand, has learned to not depend on others; on the surface he seems self-assured and confident. He doesn't worry as much about whether he is keeping all the commandments like Shannon does. This facade of self-assurance was very appealing to Shannon while they were dating, and she still asks herself why she can't be more like David. Unfortunately, modeling herself after David won't help Shannon; David is just the other side of the coin of insecure attachment. He almost never shares his struggles, hopes, or fears, with anyone, and isn't sure that this is even appropriate. He thinks people ought to stop complaining and just do what needs to be done. He is quite lonely, though, and secretly yearns to be closer to Shannon, and be more like other couples he sees who can talk about anything. The emotional and physical costs of David's form of insecurity may well become lethal; husbands who are disconnected do not gain the proven benefits that come from healthy relationships, such as better emotional and physical health, better job performance, and more joy. Their life spans are shorter, their stress levels are higher, and they usually struggle with a wide variety of health problems.

In terms of their sexual relationship, the dynamics are the same. Shannon doesn't feel attractive, worries that she isn't a very good lover, and has never given serious thought to what her sexual needs are. As a result she is very uncomfortable being nude in front of her husband, nor does she initiate any talk about their sexual relationship because she is afraid to hear that something might not be going well—and this would just reconfirm her feelings of inadequacy. David has similar insecurities, and has never expressed in any direct ways what he likes or dislikes sexually. In fact early in their relationship, they established the "normal" way to be sexual, and have pretty much repeated the same behaviors in the same places since.

On one rare occasion, however, Shannon decided to take a risk because she had learned that husbands often like more variety. But when they tried the new sexual position and it didn't work very well (since new positions typically take a little practice), she assumed that David disapproved. In reality, though, David was pleased to break out of the monotony, as it was exciting; but he reached orgasm much faster than he wanted and before Shannon could enjoy herself, so really, he was disappointed with himself. Unfortunately, he hasn't had the courage to tell Shannon that he would like to try new things again, so they returned to the same old ways. We see that because of their insecurities they aren't able to trust each other, which keeps them from candidly discussing their sexual relationship, and which handicaps their enjoyment and drains their sexual strength.

David's problem with pornography isn't really related to the quality of their sexual relationship. He has occasionally dabbled in pornography since he was a teenager and found some magazines at a friend's house, but it isn't something that would be classified as a pornography addiction. Every once in awhile he looks at things that aren't appropriate, but he doesn't try to justify it, always feels badly afterwards, and doesn't repeat the behavior for months or years at a time. He was deeply humiliated when Shannon found out about it; he lost his temper more to avoid talking about it than because he was angry at her. Deep down he really yearns to talk about the issue with Shannon, and thinks it might be helpful; but he isn't sure he can handle how upset she would be if they did talk about it, and how she might take it personally.

Because David tries to avoid thinking about these issues or discussing his feelings about them, he probably won't be as sensitive as he otherwise could be to the times when temptations may increase and he may be more likely to falter again. He just puts it out of his mind and exerts willpower to stay in control; the next time life becomes overwhelming, or he gets tired and lonely, he will likely make more mistakes. People with attachment avoidance are more vulnerable to counterfeit forms of intimacy like pornography; because they are so disconnected from others, their feelings of loneliness and isolation can become intense. And if they do not have relationships where they can talk about their poignant feelings, they become more susceptible to addictive types of behavior.

It is sad to consider that if Shannon and David could only be more secure and open, they could be helping each other so much more. Nevertheless, this is not something that is likely to happen spontaneously. It would take a measure of risk and vulnerability that would currently be very difficult for either of them. So what could help them feel more secure? Paradoxically, taking the risk to share more of their struggles with one another would be a good beginning. Even though using a therapist may be appropriate for a relationship of two insecure people, unless a couple keeps getting into destructive arguments when they try to risk and share, they can usually start the journey toward more emotional closeness on their own.

But this requires that both partners recognize the need to change, and that both are willing to take small risks to try to improve. David is the one who is more likely to impede this process of change, since with his avoidant style he is predisposed to pretend that everything is fine, and to avoid facing intense emotions. Shannon may be much more willing to admit that there are problems that need to be dealt with; once they start to talk about them, however, because of her strong anxieties and fears she may shut down the process.

Nevertheless small steps are within the reach of almost any couple. If David pushed himself to simply say, "Remember that time you tried a new sexual position? I really enjoyed that," they could begin, anew, to take small risks in the sexual area of their relationship, and enjoy themselves a little more. This should help them trust each other a little more, to where they can be more open in other areas of their lives.

Emotional Intimacy and Physical Intimacy

Attachment levels are directly related to the degree of emotional intimacy a couple can enjoy. The emotional intimacy or connection that partners can experience in the overall relationship across time is different than the enjoyment of a particular sexual encounter, and has little relation with orgasm. Physical intimacy and emotional intimacy are interrelated, but they are by no means synonymous. Emotional intimacy can be either the prelude to, or the result of, physical intimacy. In the stereotypic writings of experts on sexuality, some authors have described women as needing to feel close emotionally before they can fully become close sexually, and they have described men as needing physical closeness before they can become more vulnerable emotionally. But it is most likely that each person—regardless of gender—is different with regard to which type of intimacy leads to the other, and this may even change for some people over their lifespan. So the important point isn't so much whether one gender needs one type of intimacy *before* the other type, the point is to find a way for both partners to *eventually* experience both types of intimacy in each encounter.

Emotional intimacy has a similar process to sexual intimacy; it usually begins with more subtle and delicate behaviors, then intensifies until a heightened sense of connection is felt, after which a little less closeness is normal. The emotional and sexual response cycles mirror each other, even though the time frame for emotional intimacy is usually much broader—occurring over hours or days, while sexual intimacy is usually measured in minutes. So how does this all work together?

Couples often seek out positive experiences such as going out together to an enjoyable activity, and then they often feel closer and can talk more openly about their lives. As they talk more openly, and show that they care and are attentive to each other's concerns, they feel even closer. This added closeness helps them to trust each other more, and is sometimes followed by sharing even more with one another. Sometimes the things they share when they feel closer can be difficult to talk about such as insecurities, things they would like to change in their own lives or in their relationship, or challenges they may be having with their kids or in their jobs. In many ways, such sharing brings a stronger, more lasting feeling of closeness than anything else couples can do together.

So to have emotional closeness, couples need to dedicate consistent time for each other, they need to be able to talk with each other, and they need to have at least a basic level of trust. Perpetuating emotional closeness in a relationship is one of the more challenging aspects of our lives, and requires dedication and consistent effort. If couples neglect this aspect of their relationship, everything else will suffer—especially their sexual relationship.

Even though couples can engage in sexual encounters that are physically enjoyable—but devoid of any emotional closeness, the benefits of good sex are profoundly multiplied when emotional intimacy is also present. Sex can become so much more than just physical enjoyment; in some ways it is a beautiful metaphor for the complete oneness a couple can experience when combined with fresh experiences of emotional sharing and closeness.

Interestingly, most couples who draw near to each other emotionally will naturally want to consummate this closeness with physical touch and enjoyment. And just as emotional closeness can bring on physical closeness, physical closeness can also prompt emotional closeness. This is because physical closeness stirs up strong emotions for most people, and emotions are connected to powerful hormones of attachment. In other words, if couples are better at being physically close, they can use their feelings of connection after sex to risk a little more emotionally, or vice versa. Couples can start with the area they are stronger in to build closeness in the area they are weaker in.

Ideally, emotional intimacy should precede sex by many months, such that couples do not marry until they have found out whether they can become emotionally close. This ideal is rarely followed by nonreligious couples and is one of the key reasons why marriages are more fragile. Even in LDS relationships, the delicate nuances of emotional closeness can be smothered in courtships that are excessively focused on the grandiose feelings of physical arousal, even if it isn't leading to sexual intercourse. But even if the courtship is not excessively physical, if it is too short there still may not be enough time to develop—and test—emotional closeness. Curiously, LDS couples who receive spiritual confirmation about the rightness of their relationship often reduce the length of their courtship; this abbreviated time together can short-circuit the need to explore the fitness of their relationship in other important areas. If relationships are not founded on good emotional intimacy—but only on physical bonding and attachment, once the physical passions die down, there is not much left that the couple can communicate about; they are limited in their ability to support one another through the normal difficulties of life.

Regardless of whether a couple developed enough of a foundation of emotional intimacy before marriage, sex can replace real emotional intimacy if they become lazy in their relationships. This can happen to the best of couples as the routines of life take over, and they fall into a pattern of going out on their weekly date—that ends in sex—but includes precious little sharing of their emotions. Just as some couples may need to schedule sex when their lives become too busy, others may need to schedule talk time and push themselves to go beyond the normal sharing of their days and get into more important issues that can build emotional closeness. Consistent emotional closeness is one of the best ways to insure consistent sexual intimacy.

So what about Shannon and David? Can they achieve both emotional and physical intimacy? Because they are committed and loyal to each other, there is much to hope for in their relationship. Just like a new dating couple needs to build their relationship one conversation at a time, Shannon and David can begin afresh to take small risks—both emotionally and sexually. If they persist in these efforts—even though it may be difficult at times—they will feel themselves growing closer and closer, and feeling less anxious and avoidant. In addition, if they invite God to be a part of this process of regrowth and change, their path to more unity will be smoother and shorter. God will always help us when we work hard to achieve our righteous desires in humility. But He does require us to *ask* for His help (see *Bible Dictionary*, "Prayer").

Questions to Ponder:

1. *Am I secure enough in my relationship to frankly explore my sexual needs or those of my partner?*

2. *What does my emotional response cycle look like?*

3. *Am I aware of my spouse's emotions, and am I responsive to them?*

4. *When I feel emotional closeness, does it lead to sex? Are there other barriers to sexual enjoyment besides emotional closeness?*

5. *Do I tend to use sex as a substitute for emotional closeness?*

14

THE EMOTIONAL DIMENSION: AUTHENTICITY AND DIFFERENTIATION

One of the most meaningful gifts that we can give to each other is our authenticity. Authentic people express themselves outwardly with full congruence to how they feel, think, and believe internally. Until we are able to be authentic, our relationships are fake to one degree or another. It is a high challenge to achieve an authentic life, and even more challenging to find a partner with whom we can fully share our true selves.

Authenticity is a lifelong endeavor that most sincere people want for their relationships. Hopefully, most of us selected or will select a spouse because this person is easy to trust and someone with whom we can share some of our deepest feelings. This initial foundation of authenticity can set us on the right course, and take us to more profound levels of sharing and trusting as the years go by. Even if authenticity was not particularly strong at the beginning of marriage, we can all learn to become more authentic over time.

The reason authenticity is so challenging is because most of us have trained ourselves to sidestep awkward truths about ourselves or others that may make us uncomfortable. We often act in certain ways just to fit in with friends or in other settings, because we think that is how we are supposed to act; we are a bit of a chameleon. Even in our families we are often taught to say only certain nice things or to act in certain ways—just to fit in with how our family does things. In fact, we may find that it is sometimes the hardest to be authentic with those to whom we are closest, because we have developed habits of interacting that are not based on reality. Such shallow behaviors and pseudo relationships can be kept up for years before the façade finally comes tumbling down, and we are forced to see things as they really are: our relationships and our individual lives may not be doing nearly as well as we were pretending.

As discussed in the previous chapter, sometimes our attachment styles influence our authenticity. If we are insecure, we often do things that are not aligned with how we truly feel, because we are afraid that others may not like us or love us. We can be unauthentic on both extremes: we may try extra hard to be lovable—even doing things we think are wrong, or we may feign to be totally independent and pretend that we don't need others' love at all.

The sexual area is one of the most telling areas of life to see how good we are at being authentic. For instance, do we openly share with our partners what we like or do not like in the bedroom? Do we settle for the mundane because we lack the courage to express how we really feel, or what we would really like to try sexually? It is surprising that sometimes the simplest things are not shared because of our overwhelming discomfort with sexual topics. For example, maybe the way our spouse approaches foreplay is not quite what we know would get us turned on, but we let the same behaviors happen again and again because we are too embarrassed to say something. "I like it better when you touch me this way" is a simple statement, but too many people can hardly get the words out of their mouths; so they must settle for an inauthentic experience, and their potential enjoyment fades away.

There are many reasons why a person might not share their sexual needs. For example, some people may feel selfish if they ask for what they really like; others may be afraid of their partner's reactions; some have been taught that true sacrifice means never divulging what they secretly want. In other instances, people may be mortified to say anything about sex because it was such a shameful topic; or maybe people have simply stopped trying in their relationships, and just find it easier to pretend.

And finally, some people are so afraid their partner may rebuff their requests that they would rather be left unsatisfied than rejected. While there may be dozens of reasons why other people are not authentic, we ask you this: what is the reason why you are not as authentic as you would like? Identifying your own central reasons for not being authentic is very worthwhile because it will give you clues as to whether you need to work on your self-esteem, your shame about sexuality, your incorrect values, your fear of upsetting your partner, or some other aspect of your life.

By way of contrast, let's imagine a relationship where both people feel secure enough to risk asking for what they like and need sexually; where each person has the courage to try new, creative ways to make love and to try to please their partner; where each person is able to kindly challenge their partner when they feel that a certain area of their relationship needs more attention; where they are able to fully express their joy and happiness after being close physically and emotionally. Just imagine how much more fulfilling a relationship could be if it is full of authenticity.

For decades, experts on relationships have summarized the common reasons for lack of authenticity into a term they call *differentiation*. When people are less mature—or less differentiated—they are highly reactive to others, and tend to have pseudo relationships. They are rarely comfortable with expressing how they really feel about any subject, or being open in their relationships. The term *differentiation* helps explain the concepts in this chapter.

If we are mature and feel comfortable with who we are—including how we are different from others, we don't fret or spend a lot of energy trying to convince others to love us or agree with us. We have enough self-love and self-respect that we love and respect others—without which, we might desperately seek others' approval, or cutoff relationships because we are afraid of being rejected. It is curious that we are commanded to love others as we love ourselves, which implies that self-respect and self-love are prerequisites to love others.

The first step to authenticity is self-awareness, and an appreciation for our unique attributes, skills, and feelings. Repentance, obedience, and spiritual growth bring feelings of love from God; and when we feel approved by God, we won't have to look for approval from others because we feel it from within. Without such differentiation, we will probably struggle in all of our relationships because we don't have a firm foundation from which we can give to others. We share our true character in relationships, but we cannot share something we don't appreciate or have not yet acquired. This is one of the reasons why teen marriages are so much less stable than relationships which are formed later; individuals who are still immature have a very difficult time consistently loving someone else.

The road to authenticity is not complicated, but it is challenging to stay on it. This road has mile markers that each say: *Be True to Yourself in Every Interaction.* Perhaps the most obvious sign of a detour off the road of authenticity is a loss of fun and creativity in the sexual area of our relationships. Granted, most of us get comfortable in routines and need a lot of predictability to optimally function on a daily basis. If everything were always new and unfamiliar, however, we would become overwhelmed, and less able to focus on work or maintenance of home and relationships. Yet routines and predictability can also represent stagnation and wilting authenticity. Even though all marriages have normal ebbs and flows between excitement and routine—and the sexual area is not immune from these normal marital tides, without consistent awareness and effort routine becomes boring, and even the sexual area can lose its power to help couples bond and find pleasure. So ask yourself: *When was the last time I took a risk and tried something different or new in my sexual relationship?*

We want to be clear that we are not saying that couples need to be constantly looking for some new or unusual thing to do sexually—that is not the point at all. Such an endless pursuit of novelty can lead to strange and perverse experiences that are degrading to self and others, and have lead too many into forbidden paths. The point is that when sex becomes so routine and boring that couples are not growing and challenging themselves, that is the time to renew creativity and caring in their relationship.

If we use an analogy dealing with expressions of love, the principles may be more clear. Many couples share a routine of saying "I love you" each morning when they bid goodbye. There is nothing wrong or dysfunctional about such a habit, and it at least reminds them each day that they care for one another. But if this habit is the only way love is expressed, there is so much that a couple is likely missing. What about the unexpected phone call in the middle of the day, just to let them know you care? Or what about the surprise flowers that arrive for no apparent reason, other than to say "I love you and am thinking about you"? And what about the unexpected kiss full of passion and desire—rather than a quick peck on the check? Each of these are creative opportunities to bring a little spice and romance into the relationship, but are missed if all that is shared is the routine way of saying "I love you" on the way out the door.

This need to find new or creative ways to share your feelings of love also applies to the sexual area. Couples who care will recognize that they need to be occasionally creative in their sexual experiences in order to keep passion alive. Couples who are authentic will also see that there is much more to authenticity than just the element of creativity.

As challenging as it may be to be sexually creative, it is probably more difficult to confront problems that emerge in our relationships, especially sexual problems. Sexual behaviors are powerful and personal, such that one partner may enjoy a particular sexual experience, but the other may not enjoy it as much—or may even find it distasteful. To address such issues requires some courage and maturity. It is tempting to be passive aggressive and simply avoid the thing we find distasteful, but this will not lead to needed changes. To say, *I know you enjoy…, but I don't particularly like it when we do…,* can create some conflict and frustration. Yet once these authentic feelings are on the table, it is then possible to talk about what each person is experiencing, and new options for better experiences have a chance to emerge.

Sometimes the end result of such a conversation is that each partner just prefers different things sexually, like some people prefer seafood and others don't. Still, once this is clear, couples can figure out ways to meet each other's preferences, whether that means simultaneously or sequentially. You may find, however, that the honest conversation yields an entirely new sexual position or experience that soon may become the preference for both partners.

One of the quiet strengths about long-term committed relationships is that couples have time to mature and grow together over the years. While the physical prime of life might be in the twenties, many couples experience much more enjoyable sexual experiences after their thirties, after they have matured enough to be open with one another and let go of many of their anxieties and insecurities. After spouses let go of the idea that they are going to look like a model for the rest of their lives, it can be liberating to fully appreciate the wonders of each other's bodies—without embarrassment. In addition, as children get older and resources increase, couples can make a little more time to be alone, and rediscover what brought them together in the first place. This seasoned sexual maturity is worth waiting for. Couples who are frustrated with the demanding routines of the early years, and how their insecurities seem to keep interfering with their enjoyment, will hopefully be patient and persistent enough to keep battling against less than authentic experiences. Then later, even though they may not be sexual as often as they were during their honeymoon years, they will most likely enjoy sex at least as much—or maybe even more.

Learn to be more authentic by being more open and honest in respectful ways, and then start taking small risks. It doesn't have to be in the sexual area. The authenticity in your relationship can improve just by risking a little, or expressing a little more appreciation, or giving a small compliment of how good your partner looks in a certain outfit, or by saying how much you enjoy spending time together. Such things should also make it easier to speak a little more authentically in sexual matters. But if verbal authenticity is still hard, sometimes the easiest way to start is to guide your partner's hand to touch you in ways or in places that are more pleasing, and then show how much you enjoy this change of routine. Even though it is usually much clearer to *say* what you want (between encounters), sometimes this doesn't work very well *during* a sexual encounter, so nonverbal ways can be a simpler place to start.

It is very doubtful, however, that nonverbal hints or guidance will be enough to develop a fully authentic relationship. Talking before or after—rather than during—sexual experiences about how you want to do something a little differently can be well worth the risk. Besides, some changes you want to make are never going to be clear unless you talk about them.

The longer you have gone without being authentic, the harder it may be to start; but once started it gets easier, and the higher levels of honesty are like opening a window and letting fresh air into a room that had been filled with stale and suffocating air. Strangely, even though authenticity brings growth and more enjoyment into our relationships, it is not something that arrives and then automatically stays. In the press of daily life, we all grow a little neglectful of what is required for an authentic life, and all too soon we again find that it is hard to be open and honest in ways that keep our relationship and sexual experiences fresh and rejuvenating. So we should regularly check our authentic "barometer" to see how we are doing. A proven way to jumpstart authenticity when it has withered is to take a night away with your spouse and spend some uninterrupted time talking and sharing, both emotionally and physically.

Questions to Ponder:

1. *Am I generally authentic in what I say and in what I do in my relationship with my partner?*

2. *In what areas am I most prone to avoid being direct and open with my partner? What keeps me from being open in these areas?*

3. *Consider sharing with your partner your response to question #2; focus on what makes it more difficult for you to be open—rather than on your partner's contributions to the problem.*

4. *If you were to consider taking a small step toward more authenticity, what might it be? Will you commit to take this step? If not, what could be impeding you from making this commitment?*

15

THE SPIRITUAL DIMENSION: SEXUAL CLEAVING

After nearly three decades of research on married couples, there is one particular discovery that has been replicated by many experts: what distinguishes marriages that succeed from those that do not is not the *amount of differences* in the relationship, rather it is *the way that differences are handled*. While this is true of marriage generally, it is perhaps most true of a couple's sexual relationship specifically.

Consider another research discovery: nearly 70 percent of the differences in a couple's relationship can be labeled as *perpetual*, meaning that these differences never go away or change—they are an ongoing part of the relationship. Both happily and unhappily married couples have such *perpetual differences*. This infers that many of the differences in marriage are natural, normal, and can even be healthy, and should not be labeled as *problems*. If couples label their sexual *differences* as *problems*, they may think that the best way to resolve their issues is by getting rid of these differences. This type of thinking leads too many husbands to believe that "if my wife was more like me, we'd have a better sex life," and too many wives to think that "if my husband was more like me, I'd be more satisfied with our sexual intimacy." This "resolve-the-problem" approach to sexual differences is misdirected, and will make true intimacy difficult to achieve. In fact, such an approach will almost surely result in what experts call *marital gridlock*, a condition that is hurtful and even destructive to a couple's relationship. The healthier approach, however, is to establish a *gentle dialogue* about those perpetual differences, one that communicates openness, acceptance, affection, and collaboration.

Cleaving and the Marriage Covenant

Couples who view their marriages as a sacred covenant between them and the Lord, should have the depth of commitment that is needed to patiently work through their challenges. Honoring our marriage covenants includes following the Lord's pattern for how couples should listen to and respond to each other's needs; it also includes understanding the true principles of what marriage is—and isn't, and which people are part of the covenant. We typically define a *covenant* as a sacred agreement between two people: ourselves and God. When we are baptized, confirmed, (ordained to the priesthood), and receive our temple endowment we enter into a two-person covenant with our Father in Heaven. The marriage covenant, however, is unique because it involves three people who have covenanted with each other.

The marriage covenant is a triangular covenant—a three-way promise involving the husband, the wife, and God. Viewing marriage as a "divine triangle" should expand our understanding of the nature and meaning of the marriage covenant, and how decisions are intended to be made in marriage. In all covenants, we make promises to those with whom we covenant. In marriage, it means that we make sacred promises to God *and* our spouse. This should shift our view of marriage to what we have promised to *give*—not what we expect to *receive* from our spouse.

During the temple sealing ceremony of one of our relatives, the sealer taught a lasting lesson about how couples should view the promises they make when they are married. This temple sealer admonished the couple to make sure they listened to the words of the ordinance correctly. During the ordinance the couple would promise to observe the *rites* associated with the celestial order of marriage. He pointedly cautioned them to not hear this word as the *rights* associated with marriage. The *rights of marriage* may tempt us to focus on what we assume we are entitled to—what we think our spouse should be doing for us. The *rites of marriage*, however, are observances and practices; they are things we do and things we keep—they are not something we receive. This wise temple sealer counseled this couple to always remember what they were promising to do for each other and their marriage.

In both ancient and modern scripture, the Lord emphasizes that the covenant of marriage is sustained as spouses commit themselves to the *doctrine of cleaving*. When He ordained marriage as the crowning act of the creation, He stated, "Therefore shall a man leave his father and his mother, and shall cleave unto his wife" (Genesis 2:24). And in latter-day revelation the Lord taught, "Thou shalt love thy wife [or husband] with all thy heart, and shalt cleave unto her [him] and none else" (D&C 42:22). The doctrine of cleaving is inseparably connected to the principle of *spousal preeminence,* meaning that our relationship with our spouse should be preeminent over all other mortal relationships; parents, children, siblings, and other family members and friends become secondary to our relationship with our own spouse. Cleaving means more than just *saying* that our spouse is the most important person in our lives; our actions should *show* that we place our spouse as the top priority in our lives.

Responsiveness to Sexual Differences

In the New Testament we gain further insight into the value of cleaving and responsiveness when dealing with sexual differences. In Chapter 15 of John's testimony we read an account of Christ's final discussion with His apostles before leaving for the Garden of Gethsemane on the Mount of Olives. Sensing their anxiety at His impending departure, Jesus taught them how they could continue to have His peace and joy in their lives. He said,

> *If ye keep my commandments, ye shall abide in my love; even as I have kept my Father's commandments, and abide in His love. These things have I spoken unto you, that my joy might remain in you, and that your joy might be full. This is my commandment, that ye love one another, as I have loved you. Greater love hath no man than this—that a man lay down his life for his friends* (John 15: 10–13).

In these verses, Jesus invites his disciples to follow his pattern of loving discipleship by giving of ourselves for the good of others. We should be able to see that this pattern of responsiveness and sacrifice particularly applies to our covenant relationship with our spouse, who should also be our closest friend in life.

The Savior also shares a paradox of gospel living. A paradox is a statement that seems self-contradictory at first, but in reality expresses a truth. We live in a world where most people believe that happiness comes by focusing on our own needs, but Christ teaches that we are happiest when we carefully give a high priority to the needs of others—particularly the needs of our spouse and family members. True happiness comes into our lives because of our natural desire to connect with others—to love and be loved. The Savior emphasized that if individuals seek to "find" or "save" their own lives, they will ultimately lose them, whereas those who give a high priority to others' needs in a process of "losing" their lives, will—paradoxically—find true happiness and growth.

While the scriptural language of laying down one's life invokes images of Christ's sacrifice for each of us, and times where people actually die to save others, most of us do not respond in such dramatic ways. Following the Savior's example and overcoming self-centeredness more often involves laying down our lives for those we love one piece at a time—moment by moment, day by day—rather than in one grand gesture. In marriage, almost every day brings opportunities for spouses to unselfishly respond to each other. And note that it is the differences between spouses that create such rich developmental conditions.

When Differences Become Disagreements

As spouses strive to develop the attribute of responsiveness, they would do well to reframe how they see differences in their relationship: differences are not problems—they are opportunities. So when your partner expresses a complaint or frustration with your relationship, this then gives you an opportunity to be responsive to his or her needs and desires. Plus, when you unselfishly do something for your partner that you would not do for yourself, you express a powerful form of love. Marriage researchers Dr. Linda Waite and Dr. Maggie Gallagher have stated that selfless intimacy can

> *...literally double your sexual pleasure: you get satisfaction not only from your own sexual response but from your partner's as well..., love and concern for one's partner shifts the focus away from the self in a sexual relationship and toward the other person. This selfless approach to sex, paradoxically, is far more likely to bring sexual satisfaction to both men and women* (The Case For Marriage, 2000, p. 89).

Natural differences and occasional conflicts provide us with opportunities to be truly responsive and selfless toward our spouse. If both partners do this, they can achieve much deeper and more meaningful levels of intimacy. This is a key step in becoming eternal companions, to change and grow and become a better fit to what our spouses need.

We have observed that developing deeper levels of responsiveness takes time and extends over the course of marriage. This happens not only as spouses share life experiences and come to know each other in more authentic ways, it also happens as spouses mature, and become more anxious to respond to each other's needs and desires. But the passage of time by itself will not automatically make couples more responsive. Couples should dedicate adequate amounts of time to fostering sexual intimacy in their day to day lives. Certain types of sexual disclosure and encounters simply will not happen if time is not set aside for them. Our experience is that most couples readily understand the need for such blocks of time with respect to fostering emotional intimacy, but they sometimes fail to appreciate that the same is also true of sexual intimacy. In other words, some conversations require long, uninterrupted time to get to the heart of deep, emotional matters; likewise, in order to develop deep sexual intimacy, some encounters may take similar amounts of time.

Questions to Ponder:

1. *Do I see our differences as an opportunity to increase intimacy? Am I resentful when my spouse doesn't see things the same way I do?*

2. *Do I include God in our sexual decision making process?*

3. *Where are my spouse's sexual needs on my priority list?*

4. *Do I feel joy in meeting my spouse's needs, or resentful?*

16

THE SPIRITUAL DIMENSION: SEXUAL DECISION MAKING

A significant aspect of healthy sexuality is proper decision making patterns for both spouses. Each of the couples introduced in Chapter One are asking important questions about sexuality in their marriages that are connected to decision making. Jenny and Steve need to find consensus and make decisions about the frequency of their sexual intimacy. Alex and his wife are exploring possible decisions about specific sexual practices, while Shannon and her husband are addressing boundaries and openness about sexual matters. Joshua and his wife are making decisions about how to teach their children about sexuality in dating and marriage. While there is important information available that can help couples be better informed, *how* you make decisions as a couple is just as important as *what* you decide.

We want our decisions about how we express ourselves sexually to meet with God's approval. That is why the spiritual dimension of our sexual nature is particularly relevant to couple decision making. Our Father in Heaven has provided a "divine design" (*Proclamation on the Family*, paragraph 7) or pattern for couple decision making. Specifically, this includes *who* should be involved in couple decisions about sex, *how* such decisions should be made, and *what* criteria should be considered.

Who Should Be Involved

At times, a couple may seek advice from someone *outside* their marriage for a decision they are making about their marriage. *When* we seek such counsel is a revealing indicator of whether or not we understand the nature of our marriage covenant. Elder Dallin H. Oaks has said:

> *I like to tell a young couple who are being married that in the marriage relationship they ought to look first to each other, as they do across the altar during their marriage—not first to their parents, not first to their siblings, not first to their friends, but in solving all their problems they should look first to one another* (Worldwide Leadership Training Meeting, February 9, 2008, p.12).

When we do this *first*, we are striving to cleave to one another as spouses. If we eventually do seek counsel from a bishop, parent, or any other outside person, the best pattern is to go together to talk with that person. If both spouses are present, the couple can be unified in seeking and considering such outside advice. These patterns are particularly important in matters as personal as sex. Any solicited counsel should still be prayerfully and patiently considered by both spouses before making a decision.

How Decisions Should Be Made

The *Proclamation on the Family* reads:

> *By divine design, fathers are to preside over their families in love and righteousness and are responsible to provide the necessities of life and protection for their families. Mothers are primarily responsible for the nurture of their children. In these sacred responsibilities, fathers and mothers are obligated to help one another as equal partners* (The Proclamation on the Family, paragraph 7).

These prophetic instructions teach us that marriage consists of specific, sacred responsibilities that have been divinely given to husbands/fathers (to preside, provide, and protect), and to wives/mothers (to nurture); these are intertwined by the practice of equal partnership in marriage. It is in the proper *integration of these responsibilities* that the power and purposes of the Lord are manifested. Principles such as equal partnership, presiding, and nurturing, can be properly understood only in relation to one another. Each principle is interdependent of the other principles.

Equal partnership is the preeminent and overarching principle; presiding and nurturing are subservient to equal partnership. For example, presiding cannot eclipse equal partnership. So if a husband's pattern of presiding does not reinforce his wife's sense of equal partnership within the marriage, something is not right. Even though responsibilities may differ, the Lord intends for marriage to be one of true equality and partnership. The apostle Paul declared, "Neither is the man without the woman, neither the woman without the man, in the Lord (I Corinthians 11:11). And President Gordon B. Hinckley taught:

> *In the marriage companionship there is neither inferiority nor superiority. The woman does not walk ahead of the man; neither does the man walk ahead of the woman. They walk side by side as a son and daughter of God on an eternal journey (Ensign, May 2002, p. 52).*

Any notion of hierarchy—whether by vote or choice or priesthood or any other reason—where one spouse is put above or ahead of the other is contrary to God's will.

Again, the divine triangle of marriage reflects that the ordinance of marriage includes two interdependent covenants: a covenant with God, and a covenant with our spouse. This "triangle covenant" helps us envision how a truly equal partnership can be maintained. We see that the source of authority resides *outside* both the husband and the wife; it resides with God and within the principles of the gospel. Husbands and wives stand on level ground, and so together they should prayerfully seek the will of the Lord in order to make unified decisions.

Equal Counsel and Equal Consent

President Howard W. Hunter taught a pattern of marital decision making that includes both equal counsel and equal consent:

> *A man who holds the priesthood accepts his wife as a partner in the leadership of the home and family with full knowledge of and full participation in all decisions relating thereto. Of necessity there must be in the Church and in the home a presiding officer. By divine appointment, the*

> *responsibility to preside in the home rests upon the priesthood holder.*
> *The Lord intended that the wife be a helpmeet for man* ["meet" means
> "equal"]—*that is, a companion equal and necessary in full partnership.*
> *Presiding in righteousness necessitates a shared responsibility between*
> *husband and wife; together you act with knowledge and participation*
> *in all family matters* (Ensign, November 1999, p. 49).

Notice President Hunter's emphasis on "full knowledge," "full participation," and "full partnership" between husbands and wives in "all decisions" relating to family matters. He also taught that a *helpmeet* is very different than a *help mate*. Meet means equal, and such equality is the essence of a true partnership. Other Church leaders have also stressed the need for both equal counsel and equal consent in the marriage partnership. Speaking to husbands, President Boyd K. Packer taught:

> *When there is a family decision to be made that affects everyone, you*
> *and your wife together will seek whatever counsel you might need, and*
> *together you will prayerfully come to a unified decision. If you ever pull*
> *priesthood rank on her you will have failed* (Quoted by C. Broderick
> in *One Flesh, One Heart: Putting Celestial Love Into Your Temple*
> *Marriage*, 1986, p. 32).

The Lord's pattern of marital decision making involves husbands and wives prayerfully coming to a unified decision—unified with each other and unified with the Lord.

Proper Sources of Revelation

Most of the common questions we are asked by young adults and couples are inquiries about Church doctrine on specific aspects of marital sexuality. They want to know the "Church's official stance" on a certain sexual practice, or other specific aspect of marital sexuality. Examples include: *"What is the Church's official stance on oral sex?;" "Does the Church approve of wearing lingerie?;"* and *"Do you have to put your temple garments back on right after sex, or is it all right to sleep together naked after sex?"*

It is very common for couples to express that they have been searching for the official church position related to their question, but they haven't been able to find one. We often respond that there are general principles that have been revealed by prophets that couples should seriously consider when making personal marital decisions, but rarely is there an official church position or doctrine that directs couples in the specifics of such intimate issues. As the Doctrine and Covenants teaches, "These things remain with you to do according to judgment and the directions of the Spirit" (D&C 62:8). It is important to note that this is the same pattern the Church wants us to use for questions regarding birth control and family planning, frequency of temple worship, specifics of Sabbath day observance, calculation of tithing, time spent in church callings, and other specific aspects of personal and family decision making. The Prophet Joseph Smith said, "I teach them correct principles and they govern themselves."

Even though there may be some Church teachings or information from professionals that can inform a couple's decision making around the specifics of their marital sexuality, hoping to find an official stance of the Church on these matters reveals that they believe that the answers lie outside of—rather than within—their relationship. Couples should have confidence that the best answers to such specific questions come from *within* their relationship rather than *outside* of it. By first "turning toward" each other, spouses are more responsive and attentive, and can make wiser choices that are based on their own personal needs, desires, and experiences rather than by using outside comparisons. Such introspection as a couple places the focus on *motives* and *intents* of their sexual desires and expressions—not just *behaviors*; they consider *what* they want to do, but they should also consider *why* they want to do it.

In a recent general conference address, Elder Dallin H. Oaks encouraged church members to use proper sources of revelation in their personal decision-making.

> *The **personal** line is of paramount importance in personal decisions and in the governance of the family. Unfortunately, some members of our church underestimate the need for this direct, personal line. Responding to the undoubted importance of prophetic leadership—the **priesthood** line, which operates principally to govern heavenly communications on Church matters—some seek to have their priesthood leaders make personal decisions for them, decisions they should make for themselves by inspiration through their personal line. Personal decisions and family governance are principally a matter for the personal line...*
>
> *We must use both the personal line and the priesthood line in proper balance to achieve the growth that is the purpose of mortal life. If personal*

> *religious practice relies too much on the* **personal** *line, individualism erases the importance of divine authority. If personal religious practice relies too much on the* **priesthood** *line, individual growth suffers. The children of God need both lines to achieve their eternal destiny. The restored gospel teaches both, and the restored Church provides both (Ensign, Nov. 2010, pp. 83-86, emphasis added).*

Marital sexuality is perhaps the ultimate example where decisions should be primarily guided by the inspired personal line. As sex educators and therapists, our experience indicates that too many young adults and married couples are seeking to have priesthood leaders—whether living or dead—make these personal decisions for them. Couples should foster a pattern of making personal decisions within the divine triangle of their marriage. They would be wise to focus on the reasons and motives of their proposed choices, and avoid seeking a one-size-fits-all prescribed model of marital sexuality that has purposely never been given by our prophetic leaders. These types of decisions are best left between the husband and the wife, as they counsel with the Lord.

This personal—even private—approach to decision making strongly infers that couples should also maintain proper boundaries around the specifics of their marital sexuality. Making comparisons with other couples is rarely helpful. We cannot think of any good that could come from learning about the specifics of sex in other people's marriages—they are not you. In fact, learning about the details of other's sexuality patterns may be detrimental to a couple's sexual relation-ship as it may influence them to mimic those patterns, rather than be responsive to the needs and desires of one another. Almost nothing else is as personal and private as your sexual preferences and patterns. Therefore, your sexual relationship should be tailored to your spouse, and not influenced by outside expectations or comparisons.

Principles of Sexual Decision Making

We close this chapter by suggesting four principles of sexual decision making in marriage. Each is paired with a key question couples can discuss. Each principle and question can be used when considering a specific sexual decision or a specific encounter, when examining broader sexual patterns in the relationship.

Principle 1: Marital Unity

Does this strengthen our relationship with each other and with God?

As we discussed in Chapter Three, the two divine purposes of sex are procreation and the strengthening of unity between spouses. If spouses focus on this in their sexual expressions with each other, they can reinforce their alignment with God and His plan of happiness. The image of the divine triangle should inspire couples to make *unity* the primary focus of their sexual expressions. At times, marital unity can be strengthened by sexual exploration, creativity, fun, passion, and enjoyment in seeing the sexual responses in our own body as well as our spouse's body. At other times, however, unity can be strengthened by sexual restraint, where spouses share emotional or non-arousing forms of intimacy, rather than arousing sexuality.

Principle 2: Couple Consensus

Do we agree on this aspect of our marital sexuality?

The divinely prescribed principles of *cleaving* and *equal partnership* obligate couples to seek a mutually agreeable and mutually satisfying pattern of sexuality in their marriages. Spouses should never manipulate or try to force their partner to engage in anything sexual with which they are not comfortable, or to which they do not consent. Spouses should try to understand the differences in their sexual preferences, and make decisions that champion their spouse's happiness and preferences, and not just their own. This principle places a high premium on communication—both during and after sex—where couples can negotiate and find consensus on specific aspects of their intimacy.

Principle 3: Positive Attitudes

Does this reflect a positive and healthy attitude about sexuality?

When differences about sexuality arise in a marriage, one or both spouses may question why they are uncomfortable with, or do not desire, something that their partner desires. So when this happens, it is enlightening if spouses try to identify the *origin* of their discomfort or their lack of desire. Sometimes these different preferences are merely situational, such as not being in the mood, or feeling tired, sick, or preoccupied; and other differences may be more lasting. Many spouses have acquired rather negative attitudes about sexual expression that may have started years earlier in family experiences, or from other sources prior to or outside of their marriage. Such differences may also be tied to healthy inhibitions or unhealthy inhibitions. *Healthy inhibitions* are connected to a spouse's personal preferences for sexual experience, and also reflect his or her values about sexuality. Healthy inhibitions are balanced by otherwise positive attitudes about sexuality, and a general willingness to engage in desired forms of sexual encounters and arousal. *Unhealthy inhibitions* are usually expressions of negative sexual conditioning which originated from past experiences or from external influences—rather than genuine personal preferences. Spouses with unhealthy inhibitions tend to avoid creativity in sexual encounters, and are often uncomfortable with their own sexual response—regardless of the specific type of arousal or stimulation.

Principle 4: Sexual Potential
Does this foster the sexual needs of my spouse and myself?

In sexual decision-making, couples should accept that the truth that some sexual preferences originate from innate sexual *needs*—not just personal desires. As we have highlighted in our model of sexual wholeness, our innate sexual nature gives each of us the capacity and desire for meaningful sexual experiences. In a marriage, each spouse individually, as well as the couple itself, has a divinely created *sexual potential*; healthy sexuality is fostered when spouses seek to share such sexual potential together. This process requires openness, vulnerability, and creativity in learning to share the sexual part of themselves with one another. This becomes a significant contributor to a rich, whole, and satisfying marriage.

Questions to Ponder:
1. *How do I maintain the "rites of marriage" within my relationship?*
2. *How is my partnership based on equality? Do we counsel with each other on family issues, and give our consent and support to the final decision?*
3. *Is our personal decision making done within the context of the divine triangle?*
4. *Do I tend to make sexual decisions based on true principles or on situational whims?*

17

STRIVING FOR SEXUAL WHOLENESS

This is the last chapter before we address specific questions people have asked about sexuality. Before we make this transition we want to summarize and give a few remaining principles. We have presented a comprehensive model about sexuality, a new way of thinking designed to help you and your partner progress in your sexual functioning. The areas that influence this range from the spiritual to the physical and the emotional. Perhaps you are beginning to understand why sexual functioning is more challenging and complex—but also more rewarding—than any of us may have imagined when we were first married.

It can be useful for couples to regularly reconsider these three areas of sexual wholeness, and talk about what is working well and what could be improved. Be careful though, as it is easy to overanalyze sexuality, and this is one part of life where being spontaneous and having fun is so essential. If your evaluations are getting in the way of the fun and pleasure, you may need to set it aside for a season and just enjoy yourselves. In other words, we do not want to leave you with the impression that you need a graduate degree to understand sex or a therapist to help you achieve the levels of intimacy you desire. The two things you most need to achieve true intimacy are a body and a committed marriage relationship with someone you love. And the Lord's plan for our happiness is all about each of us receiving both!

Beyond those two primary things, the key attribute for developing sexual wholeness is your dedication and sustained effort. What we so often find when couples have grown distant or sexually dissatisfied is that it all started with simple neglect, usually from busy schedules and a slow erosion of sex as a priority in their relationship. Such neglect easily creeps in for most of us during our marriages.

Remember that you have made a sacred covenant to give yourselves to each other and become one. This covenant is the most far-reaching covenant you can make in this life, and it has been sanctioned by God. Nothing should consistently take priority over this covenant except your relationship with God, and we believe that usually your relationship with God and your spouse are indivisible. In this area the Bible is clear:

> *For this cause shall a man leave father and mother, and shall cleave to his wife: and they twain shall be one flesh. Wherefore they are no more twain, but one flesh. What therefore God hath joined together, let not man put asunder* (Matthew 19: 5–6).

We should prioritize our relationship with our spouse so that we become of one heart, one mind, one body; all else is secondary—even our extended families. Nobody or no thing has the right to put asunder this relationship. Children, church callings, jobs, parents, entertainment, hobbies, friends, fame, or fortune—none of this should be allowed to put distance in a marriage relationship. Neither should personality conflicts, differences, or moods of the two people who have made this covenant with each other and God. There should be an almost weekly accounting of how we are doing in this relationship or the distance may grow. Sustained effort on many fronts is important in marriage, and sustained effort in sexual unity is an apt barometer of how we are doing in the entire marriage since this can demand more of us physically, emotionally, and spiritually than any other area if we want our intimacy to be fulfilling. One overlooked benefit of being in a relationship is that there are *two* people to guard your relationship, who will protect boundaries to keep neglect at bay. If both partners regularly consider how their relationship is doing, things are much less prone to grow distant. Something is amiss if only one partner takes most of the responsibility for keeping the romance alive.

Nevertheless, we should accept—even expect—that there may often be substantial struggles in the area of sexuality. In some ways, maintaining oneness in this area is a moving target because it is so deeply interrelated with everything else, including our health, our moods, our stress, etc. Furthermore, we are not the same people today that we were even just a year ago; our covenants have not changed but our world has, and we may need to change with it and make adjustments. Since there seems to always be degradation and decay in everything around us—even in our bodies, making adjustments can be frustrating, but there is beauty in the struggle. Besides, changes in our relationships over time are just as likely to bring surprising positive outcomes as they are to bring negative ones. Then, as time goes by, we often let go of some of our unfruitful hang-ups or anxieties and are better able to enjoy our relationships. As each couple struggles to stay united through the natural ups and downs of life, they earn more appreciation for each other and deeper feelings of love. There are priceless gifts that come with enduring to the end—together.

A metaphor from sports may be illustrative. We marvel when we see a team from modest beginnings grow and develop trust and confidence in each other. They find a way to mesh their individual talents into an effective unit and build esprit de corps. These special teams amaze us as they go on to have undefeated seasons, break world records, or reach heights that were thought impossible. Just witnessing this motivates us to work harder to be more exceptional ourselves. Sadly yet inevitably, winning streaks end, nearly every record is broken, and sometimes even the most united teams fall into bickering and divisiveness. Yet it is these very ups and downs that make the extraordinary times so enjoyable. If every season produced an undefeated team, or old records were broken year after year, we would not feel nearly as much excitement or joy in such achievements. It is the exceptional nature of these achievements that makes them so compelling and gratifying. In like manner, exceptional moments of unity and love in our relationships may frame our lives, or be a small element in the foreground of our "painting," but they do not make up the background of the painting. The background is full of the mundane and regular routines of living that are usually far from being intimate or thrilling. Nevertheless, extraordinary encounters or seasons are welcome reminders of what can still be achieved in this telestial world, and what can be hoped for more consistently in the life to come.

For some couples it may seem that such special moments of unity are never reachable. For others, they were reachable in times past, but now seem to be so elusive that hope is hard to maintain. Each couple walks their own unique journey; some may achieve most of the best they will experience early on; others may have notable times scattered throughout the years; and still others may be united and happy almost always. Still, very few couples are completely spared from hard times and hard years, and all must eventually deal with loss. The greatest blessings for

for enduring to the end are not to be awarded in this life. It would not be called *enduring* if it did not sometimes stretch us to our limits. Importantly, everyone can improve from today forward with persistent effort and through the healing and enabling power of the Atonement of Jesus Christ.

There are some couples who face what seem to be insurmountable challenges, including loss of physical capacities in the sexual area, unexpected trauma, tragedy, depression, or pain. God's grace and Christ's Atonement are particularly suited to help us during these trials when we do all we can do but still come up short of our potential and desires. Even though we may lose capacities in one area of life, God's grace, along with the Law of Compensation, extends to us understanding and help in another area—the area that "passeth all understanding." The power of the Atonement is not a panacea that will magically cause all difficulties to disappear, but the promises are sure that the Lord will give us real comfort and undeniable peace. Such peace and comfort comes when the Lord knows it will do us the most good and have the longest benefit—if we will allow it. Some of our most serious suffering comes as a result of missed opportunities in our relationships, or from decisions we wish we could have back. Sometimes this includes struggles in the sexual area, and we should seek healing in this area of our relationship just as much as any other area of family life.

We should see it as a great blessing to have each other—imperfections notwithstanding, and to be in partnership with the Lord who can make up for our weaknesses. However, we should come unto Him when we are frustrated with our weaknesses, and not turn our frustrations toward our partner. Only the Lord can make weak things become strong, or separated hearts become one. There is a certain nobleness in honest struggle, and compensatory blessings to the struggling that those who give up prematurely will never know.

Questions to Ponder:

1. *Do I participate in a weekly accounting for the health of our relationship?*

2. *How can I seek for healing in my sexual life?*

3. *Do I acknowledge missed opportunities, and genuinely try to overcome weaknesses in my sexual life?*

SECTION III

QUESTIONS ABOUT SEXUALITY

18

QUESTIONS ABOUT SEXUAL NORMS & SEXUAL RULES

In this final section of the book we answer common questions about sexuality that we have been asked during our professional careers. This is our way of teaching you how the general principles we have presented can be applied to specific relationship questions and concerns.

Some of the most common questions have to do with "What is normal?" People want to know whether their circumstances are normal, or whether they may have a real problem that needs attention. Here are some questions that fit this type of concern:

> 1. I feel like being sexual only once a week or so, but my partner feels like being sexual three to four times a week. Is this normal? Or should I be figuring out what is wrong with me because I don't want sex as often as my partner?

> 2. Since we have several children now and our lives are busy, we seem to find time for sex only once a week. While this seems to be enough for both of us, I wonder if we are neglecting this area of our relationship and could end up regretting something. What do you think?

> 3. We have found one or two ways of being sexual together that work really well for us, so that is what we do every time. Sometimes when I read articles that talk about all the different sexual positions I wonder

if we are missing out, but what we do is really fun and always works. Should we be more creative? We have tried a few different things in the past, but nothing seems to work as well as our "normal" way. Is my spouse going to get bored with me if we are not experimenting with different positions and such?"

Sexual Norms

Before we address these questions, we want to present some data we have collected about LDS couples, and then discuss a few principles about sexual norms. The following two tables about sexual norms for *interest in* and *frequency of* sex for married LDS men and women come from the RELATE dataset at *www.relate-institute.org.*

Table 18.1		
"How often would you like to have sex with your partner?" (As answered by married LDS females and males)		
Response	**Females**	**Males**
0. *Never*	1 %	0 %
1. *Less than once a month*	4 %	2 %
2. *1 - 3 times a month*	13 %	5 %
3. *Once a week*	21 %	12 %
4. *2 - 4 times a week*	43 %	46 %
5. *5 - 7 times a week*	15 %	27 %
6. *More than once a day*	3 %	8 %
Mean	*3.6*	*4.17*
Standard Deviation	*1.17*	*1.03*

Table 18.2		
"How often do you have sex with your partner?"		
(As answered by married LDS females and males)		
Response	**Females**	**Males**
0. *Never*	4 %	3 %
1. *Less than once a month*	4 %	5 %
2. *1 - 3 times a month*	15 %	16 %
3. *Once a week*	22 %	23 %
4. *2 - 4 times a week*	40 %	38 %
5. *5 - 7 times a week*	13 %	12 %
6. *More than once a day*	2 %	3 %
Mean	*3.35*	*3.35*
Standard Deviation	*1.28*	*1.26*

The first thing you may notice from these tables is that married LDS women desire less frequent sex than married LDS men. You may also notice as you compare the data that "normal" isn't as easy to define as might be expected. Most behaviors—even in marriage—fall into a pattern called the *bell curve*, as illustrated in Figure 18.3. This figure illustrates how a population is distributed across a specific behavior or attribute. This bell curve could just as well have been about intelligence, athletic capacity, femininity, masculinity, or other common characteristics or behavior. Even though the shape of the curve might be a little different for each concept, for example one curve might be narrower with a higher peak, or another might be wider with a shorter peak, in general they would all look somewhat like a bell. A bell curve is what telestial life looks like. Human bodies, minds, and emotions vary along a continuum, with the majority being in the middle. So although the majority of the married LDS women and men who answered these questions have sex between a few times a month to a few times a week, it is still "normal" for people to be distributed across the breadth of this bell curve.

How might this knowledge help couples? If a person wants sex daily or more often, it may indicate that they are unusually interested in sex compared to the rest of the world, but they are still normal in that they fall under this bell curve.

Table 18.3

Sexual Interests of Married LDS Couples
How often LDS couples would like to have sex with their partner

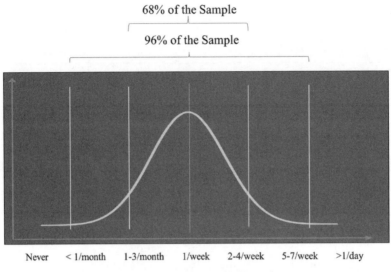

How often LDS couples would like to have sex

They may not be average, but they are still normal. Regardless of whether they are average or normal, does this change the reality of what the individual or couple needs to address?

Normal is an elusive concept and does not really change the fact that a spouse needs to deal with their own particular interest level, as well as differences in interest levels as a couple. Sometimes this means that a person is sexual less often than they want, while others are sexual more often than they want. It is as unrealistic to expect both spouses to have the same level of interest in sex as it is for them to have the same level of interest in any other activity. Each couple has to discover what is normal for them, and try to maximize their enjoyment and love while taking into consideration each partner's preferences.

As you can now see, most questions about what is normal are not usually answerable or helpful to ask. The exception to this may be when you are trying to identify whether there is a serious physical or emotional issue that is interfering with your sexual life. For example, couples may occasionally have sexual struggles that require medical or therapeutic assistance. And perhaps medicine can help if there is some underlying physical or hormonal problem that is increasing or decreasing the sexual desire to unmanageable levels.

Sexual Rules

As we discussed briefly in previous chapters, another common type of question asked by many LDS couples deals with what is okay or acceptable in terms of sexual behaviors, thoughts, and feelings within marriage. While we will address each of these in more detail in forthcoming chapters, a few principles and answers can be presented here that might help with questions about sexual rules. LDS individuals who have testimonies of the Gospel have found that keeping the commandments brings great peace and happiness. It is natural, then, that they would also want to know the commandments and laws about sexual behaviors so they can avoid making mistakes that might result in the loss of the Spirit or undermine their treasured relationships.

Here are few questions that suggest these people are concerned about sexual rules:

A. Is there anything written by prophets or apostles about which sexual behaviors are appropriate in marriage, and which are not? It would be nice to have some guidelines to make sure we aren't making mistakes.

B. My partner likes to be naked all the time. We don't have any children so it isn't a matter of other people seeing us, but I wonder about the commitment to wear our garments both night and day. Or am I just too uptight about these things?

C. My friend told me that the Bible says we shouldn't have sex on Fast Sundays. Is that true?

D. I don't seem to naturally think about sex very often, but when I do it is enjoyable and fun to think of being sexual with my partner. I have also found that reading a romance novel or watching a "chic flick" can help get me in the mood. Is that inappropriate? My partner doesn't seem to mind just as long as it gets me in the mood.

E. We don't agree on birth control, and it is affecting our sexual relationship. I believe that any form of birth control, short of abortion, is fine as long as we are having children and not being selfish about it. My partner, however, thinks that we should just let God decide when we have children, and that we shouldn't use anything artificial. But I find myself reluctant to be sexual when I know I am fertile because I'm not yet ready to have another baby. Who is right?

Individuals could spend hours searching for what Church leaders have said about each of these issues. Almost always, what they will find is that General Authorities do not get specific about such things because these are decisions that couples should make on their own. Maybe that is another reason why they are called *general* authorities—not *specific* authorities. In general, the scriptures and Church authorities have indicated that such things as adultery, fornication, and pornography are inappropriate, and they have not attempted to prescribe specific rules beyond that for married partners.

As we explained in Chapter 16, these are issues under the *personal* line of authority rather than the *priesthood* line of authority. It would be just as inappropriate to let a church authority make these decisions for a couple as it would be for the couple to make decisions about a ward or stake if such was not within their direct stewardship.

Nevertheless, we have noticed that couples can still make some serious errors when they are addressing questions that are under their personal line of authority—especially about sexuality. Some couples claim an "anything goes" attitude, while others maintain a "nothing goes" attitude. For example, the commitment to wear sacred garments both night and day is not defined specifically in terms of sexual activities by any general authority of whom we are aware. Consequently, couples will need to decide what their stance will be about nudity.

It seems reasonable to assume that sexual activities are the types of activities, like swimming, where garments can be appropriately removed. But what is a sexual activity? Is it only the few minutes during the sexual act? Or could it include extensive foreplay, or time together leading up to sexual acts? Couples who are more stringent may feel uncomfortable with any nudity, which can seriously interfere with appropriate sexual activities and interest.

On the other hand, couples who are more indulgent might interpret this to mean that the only time they need to wear clothes is when they leave the house, probably stretching the meaning of *sexual activity* to the other extreme of what is reasonable. In many cases, one partner may be markedly more or less conservative than the other, creating interesting challenges for the couple. Yet these differences should be seen as an opportunity to learn to take two perspectives, two backgrounds, two personalities—and make them one. This does not necessarily mean that both partners will see or interpret things exactly the same, but it should mean that they can make a unified decision that tries to honor both people and the principles they believe in. Accomplishing this is no small challenge!

Each couple should be aware of their own tendencies towards liberal or conservative interpretations of issues, and discuss with each other what they feel is appropriate. It is also crucial that they are prayerful, thoughtful, and respectful of each other's biases; it is all too easy to make each other feel ashamed or disrespected because of our different attitudes and upbringing. Finally, once a joint decision is reached, they should reevaluate their decision if either one has persistent feelings of discomfort.

Answering a Specific Question

Having gone through many preliminaries, you may have noticed that we have yet to directly answer any of the questions posed at the start of this chapter. Drawing on the principles from this chapter and those presented in Chapter 16 entitled "Principles of Sexual Decision Making," we will now demonstrate how a couple might work together to develop a specific answer to their personal questions about sexuality.

We will start by addressing the first question mentioned in this chapter:

> *I feel like being sexual only once a week or so, but my partner feels like being sexual three to four times a week. Is this normal? Or should I be figuring out what is wrong with me because I don't want sex as often as my partner?*

First, who do you think asked this question, the husband or the wife? In this instance it was the husband. Do you think this is normal? Even if we said it is not normal for the husband to want sex less than the wife, does it matter? This couple needs to figure out what to do with their discrepancy in sexual interest—regardless of whether or not they are considered normal. We can think of only two reasons why worrying about whether this particular issue is normal might be helpful. First, if we know that it is normal to be having certain problems, sometimes this makes us feel less distressed and we then seem to handle the problems in a better way. And second, if we learn that our problems are *not* normal, this may indicate a need to look for solutions that are not so obvious, such as underlying medical problems.

Especially in the early years of marriage, it is normal for a husband to be interested in sex more than his wife. So the husband asking this question is unusual if he is young. But we need to know more information that could influence how this particular problem should be resolved. What if he is 60 years old and his wife is 45? What if he has had testicular cancer and it has affected his hormonal levels? Such additional information might change how we interpret the problem, but it would not change the fact that this couple still needs to find a workable solution.

The question, then, is how should a discrepancy in sexual interest be handled? Assuming it is not because of an illness or underlying physical problem—which is always something that should be explored with a long-standing sexual challenge, this couple can use the principles of sexual decision making to find a solution. A key benefit of using these principles is that it should help the couple avoid making impulsive or poorly thought out decisions that could lead to even worse problems down the road.

For example, an obvious and seemingly quick solution that could be considered would be for the husband to use Viagra. However, the use of medication should usually be considered later in the decision making process, or if it has been confirmed that the source of the problem is physiological. This measured and patient approach should help most couples avoid the serious side effects of medications, and allow them time to figure out the real underlying issues that are affecting their relationship.

The first principle of sexual decision making is *"Does this strengthen our relationship with each other and with God?"* Good solutions should help the couple draw nearer to each other and to God. If the couple unwisely decided either to have either the male always force himself to be sexual whenever the female wanted, or to have the female always restrain herself until her partner initiated sex, it is likely that resentment would fester, and their relationship with each other—and by definition their relationship with God—would be injured. It is likely that the couple has already tried this short-sighted "solution," and have found that they are still not happy with that arrangement. So we see that a better solution would be something where one person is not required to give in all the time.

In what might at first seem to contradict the previous paragraph, one of the things we have suggested is for the couple to conduct an experiment for two months. During the first month, one person—usually the one with more interest in sex—is given permission to be sexual with their partner as often as they want, just as long as their requests are at times where sex is reasonable and doesn't put their jobs in jeopardy or cause them to miss church, etc., because they are spending extra time in bed! During the second month, then, the other person is in charge and decides how often they will be sexual.

Ironically, what often happens when couples try this experiment is that the person who wanted sex more frequently than their partner finds out that if they can have sex whenever they want—they don't want it nearly as often as they thought. Conversely, when the other partner has their month and isn't faced with turning down sex "all the time," they discover that they want it more often than they used to.

This exercise often helps couples see that their problem is not some inherent dramatic difference in sexual interest; it is their disunity, their inattention to each other's cues and needs, and their feelings of frustration and resentment that are really creating the problem. This exercise also reveals how sexual challenges often indicate the health of the overall relationship, or it exposes underlying issues that need to be addressed.

The second principle of sexual decision making is *"Do we agree about this aspect of our sexuality?"* Obviously they do not currently appear to have the same interest in sex, but this does not mean they cannot agree on a common solution for handling this problem. Assuming this couple tries the two month experiment and finds that they are much closer than they thought in their sexual interest, the solution has to be in figuring out a way to be more attentive to each other's needs and learning to decline and accept invitations to sex in different ways.

For couples to begin to find a solution, they have to agree on the problem. The problem isn't that one person wants sex more often than the other—even if this is a fact; the real problem is that the couple has yet to learn how to handle such a discrepancy in a cooperative way that helps them grow closer together. So to reach agreement, the couple has to first find out and agree on what the real problem is, discuss possible solutions, and then choose a course that fits for both of them.

Not surprisingly, some couples who try the two month experiment we suggested earlier end up adopting it as a solution for many years. They continue to alternate each week or month who is in charge of their sexual activity. This setup works if the engagement in sexual activity is not a power struggle. For some, it begins a pattern of successes, where previously they may have felt like they were failing either because they were expecting too much from their partner or not enough from themselves. So the reason this could work for the long-term—and we are not suggesting that this is the only solution for this problem—is if *both partners agree* that is it okay for them to have different levels of interest in sex, and *both partners agree* that the solution they feel best about is to take turns on who is in charge of sexual activities during specific weeks or months.

The third principle of sexual decision making is *"Does this reflect a positive and healthy attitude about sexuality?"* Problems that arise while trying to deal with different levels of sexual interest are often the result of negative or unhealthy attitudes about sexuality. These are some examples of such unhealthy attitudes: *"We should both want sex the same amount;" "My partner must be sexually dysfunctional because he [she] doesn't want sex as often as I do,"* or conversely, *"...wants sex all the time;" "My partner should be able to automatically tell when I am not in the mood, and not even start down that road so that I won't have to reject him [her];" "My partner should be able to get turned on whenever he [she] sees that I am interested, even if we have been neglecting our relationship recently."*

This third principle of sexual decision making is usually used to evaluate whether the final proposed solution is appropriate. But we see from the previous paragraph that the very problem itself is often a result of unhealthy sexual attitudes—which need to be addressed *before* the proposed solution is evaluated. Only then is it useful to explore whether you think the solution is based on healthy, Gospel-centered principles.

So, for example, you both might decide that the solution to your different levels of interest in sexuality is to watch or read together more sexually explicit material to get both of you turned on at the same time. Obviously you would see, however, that such a solution would fall outside the boundaries established by your Church leaders, and would be offensive to the Spirit—even if it provided a "solution" that seemed to temporarily work.

The final principle of sexual decision making is *"Does this foster the sexual needs of myself and my spouse?"* Inherent in this principle is the desire to meet your spouse's needs. When differences in sexual interest becomes a problem it is often because one or both partners have turned their attention from what would make their partner happy to what would make themselves happy. And such a self-focus quickly brings feelings of resentment or frustration when your own needs are not met. Lost are caring behaviors that used to dominate your relationship, of trying to understand and meet the needs of your spouse—even if they were different from your own.

It is usually the best policy when starting to address such a lingering problem to first help your spouse feel better rather than yourself. This may mean taking care of the kids a night each week so that your spouse can have some private time for renewal. This may mean being physically close—such as taking a bath together or giving your partner a massage—but that does not lead to sex. Such nonsexual activities can send the message that you care about your partner more than just as a sex object, and may change the perception that the only physical activity you enjoy together is sex.

19

QUESTIONS ABOUT SEXUALITY BEFORE MARRIAGE: TEACHING CHILDREN ABOUT SEXUALITY

President Harry S. Truman once said, "I have found the best way to give advice to your children is to find out what they want and advise them to do it." President Truman's advice to parents may eliminate all controversies with their children, but it will probably not instill any values, nor help adolescents set and maintain high standards. A parent's duty, however, is to accomplish both. When it comes to teaching children about sexuality, their dual task of instilling values—without controversy or embarrassment—becomes that much more difficult. So it comes as no surprise that many parents struggle to discuss sexuality with their children.

Our goal as parents should be to discuss sexuality with the same confidence and poise as we discuss any other important spiritual topic. When we are given an assignment to teach on a subject we feel inadequate to teach, we seek out trustworthy sources of information, study, and ask for direction from the Spirit of the Lord. Very few children could ever say, "Wow, my parents gave me too much information on the dynamics of sex. I wish they wouldn't be so open."

On the contrary, children—especially adolescents—want more information about sex. Research indicates that most children are likely to receive information about sex from sources other than their parents. And most often these other sources are the media. Because children's ideas of sexuality are regularly influenced by the media, parents need to be all the more open and clear on their message of sexuality; parents set the tone so that children feel no embarrassment talking about not only the mechanics of sex, but also the linked spiritual and emotional dimensions of sex.

Without early and regular communication on sexuality by parents and/or church leaders, adolescents are likely more susceptible to the highly persuasive messages in movies, books, and even commercials. These sources are increasingly eager to influence what people think about sexuality. But outside media such as movies, television, magazines, novels, or the internet rarely give consistent, correct, or virtuous information.

Parents who openly answer sexual questions, and also teach the spiritual and emotional dimensions of sexuality will have a most lasting influence on the development of their children's sexual attitudes. Such open communication is especially critical to develop as other sources attempt to hijack parental values.

A teenager by name of Jordan had an experience that demonstrates this point. Jordan's parents regularly and openly discussed sex and its meaningful place in marriage. Not surprisingly, one of Jordan's athletic coaches also wanted to discuss sexual issues. During one such conversation Jordan's coach told him and a group of other players that they needed to be prepared for that "accidental" moment when they *would* have sex. The coach then gave each boy a condom to carry in his wallet. Jordan did not seek out this advice, and felt confused by his coach preparing him for an "accidental" sexual experience.

Significantly, Jordan felt comfortable raising the issue with his parents. Why? Because his parents had previously established a relationship that accommodated—even encouraged—discussions about sex. Two influential role models—parents and a coach—had dramatically different opinions on sexuality. But which opinion was right? Jordan brought up the subject with his parents the first chance he had an appropriate moment with them. His parents weren't dramatic, but reinforced the message that sex was a good thing—at the right time and under the right circumstances. It also provided them with a fortunate opportunity to also teach that the time to say *"No"* to pre- marital sex was long before finding himself in a compromising situation. Beyond that, they discussed the idea of carrying a condom in his wallet, and how it slyly sent the message that having sex outside of marriage was indeed inevitable.

If we as parents have not established an open dialogue about sexuality, we will miss opportunities to clarify messages about sexuality. Adolescents, like Jordan, will be less likely to bring up confusing messages they receive if the channel of communication on sexuality is not already open and encouraged.

Here is another example of what it means to have an open, substantive, and honest dialogue about sex. A teenage girl approached her mother one night and told her that there was going to be a party at a friend's house and that the girl planned on going. She also told her mother that a boy she liked would be there. "Great!" the mom said, "tell me more about him." The girl was happy to describe this boy's charming personality, wit, and good looks. She then asked if it was "all right" with her mom if she held hands with him. That was a sweet moment for both mother and daughter.

If we can have our children asking for our opinion on their expressions of affection, we have established a meaningful level of communication on sexuality. Parents might even talk about their daughter's feelings, and how holding this boy's hand may influence her emotions. Such is a perfect moment to listen, and share a few comments on appropriate affection.

Parent's attachment with their children affects the amount of influence they have with their children. If parents determine that they may have less than a secure attachment, they can improve it by listening more when their children talk, discerning their children's concerns, and establishing an open and respectful pattern of communication. This will build trust and improve attachment.

The most important thing for our children is our example. If children observe a healthy attitude toward sexuality in their parents' relationship, such as appropriate affection, loving communication, authentic spirituality, etc., there may be less need for lengthy discussions. Children tend to adopt parents' examples much more than parents' lectures.

Frequently Asked Questioned

We reaffirm that sexual wholeness is dependent on success in three areas: emotional, physical, and spiritual. So even when we talk about the development of sexuality before marriage, we must still address all three categories.

1. *When should I begin to talk to my child about sexuality?*

Most research encourages parents to have a beginning talk about sexuality by the time their child is eight years old. Prior to that, we can answer children's questions with as little or as much information as *they* want to know. And we can begin to help them understand the three dimensions of sexuality by connecting physical, emotional, and spiritual experiences. But by the age of eight they are generally mature enough to understand the physical nature of sex, and can begin to link that to the other two dimensions of sexuality. For other age-appropriate sexual discussion ideas, refer to Table 19.1 at the end of this chapter.

2. *How can I talk to my child about masturbation and wet dreams?*

Masturbation is when someone manipulates their own sexual organs to produce a sexual excitement, and is generally accepted by the world as a harmless way to sexually gratify oneself. Even though it is contrary to LDS teachings, the common advice of the day encourages this practice.

We can help our children understand why we are admonished not to misuse this sacred power by explaining that meaningful sexuality is more than simple physical gratification, and if we focus on just the physical gratification it will impair healthy sexual development.

Since healthy sexuality includes a combination of *shared* emotional, spiritual, and physical expressions, masturbation is a dead end because it is a *self-centered* activity. Sexual relationships are intended to create a strong emotional bond that fortifies a relationship, deepens spirituality, and provides physical pleasure. Parents can help children understand that using sexuality for personal gratification stunts the growth of healthy sexuality.

It is likely that many young men and women experience masturbation through self-exploration as their bodies mature and feelings grow stronger. If parents are having regular conversations with youth about sexuality, it should be less likely for this to occur; nevertheless, many youth may still make mistakes in this area regardless of parental efforts.

How a parent handles such mistakes can set a tone—for better or worse—on how youth view their bodies, on sexuality in general, as well as on repentance and personal growth. If a parent is abrupt or harsh, the youth may develop shame-based attitudes, or maybe even self-loathing; this can plant the seeds of depression, suicidal thoughts, or hating all sexual feelings—including those that are normal and natural. On the other hand, if parents are kind and empathetic, they can help children learn to be aware of the feelings and actions that may lead to masturbation, and encourage their self control. They will also be giving their child the gift of knowing how problems can be overcome, and in a way where self-respect can be maintained—even when their actions are out of alignment with their values. If there has been a long term issue with masturbation, it is unlikely that youth will just stop without any relapses, so parents and church leaders should patiently guide them on a path of improvement, even if complete cessation takes months or years.

We should also help children understand that having wet dreams is very different from masturbating. *Wet dreams* occur when millions of sperm that grow in the testicles within spermatic fluid are automatically released or ejaculated while a boy is asleep. This is sometimes called *nocturnal emissions and* can be accompanied by sexual dreams, but not always.

3. *How can I help my children have a better attitude toward puberty?*

There are many helpful books that include descriptions of the physical development of the body during middle adolescence, which is called *puberty*. But in addition to understanding the physical changes, it is important to understand that these physical changes bring emotional changes as well. Among other things, girls may feel heightened emotions, and boys may feel more energetic and aggressive.

During this season of rapid physical change parents can reassure adolescents, and openly talk about not only the physical and emotional changes they can look forward to, but also the maturing spiritual development they can expect. A meaningful focus of parents is to help youth understand the spiritual side of their development, alongside their physical and emotional development.

When one of our daughters was about 11 years old, she had some confusing feelings about puberty. We were going through the nightly routine and she was settling into bed. We talked for a moment about her day, and then she said, "I don't know why, but I feel so sad. Everything is going fine, but right now I feel like crying." It was a fitting opportunity to discuss how physical changes during puberty also cause emotional changes. We then discussed how such physical and emotional changes could be better understood if we saw them through spiritual glasses, and reminding her that she is a child of God and is beginning to develop the godlike power of creating life.

It can be very encouraging to see puberty as the physical change that brings with it these wonderful powers. And with that comes feelings that are exciting, rewarding, and stunningly beautiful. With care, parents can shift the view on puberty from one of dread to a realization that this is a delightful and desirable development.

It may be particularly difficult to instill such positive outlooks about puberty if children mature early and experience sexual harassment at school or in other settings, and begin to hate the insensitive comments others make about their maturing bodies. In such cases, it is even more important that children have a safe outlet to talk to trusted parents and friends who can help them counter negative attitudes about their bodies brought on by peers who may be less than mature or virtuous. Parents may even need to engage school personnel or certain parents so that the harassment can be stopped.

4. What is sexting? What's the harm in sexting?

Texting with a cell phone or computer is convenient, useful, and is the main means of communication for many people. Some parents and children use texting to keep in touch throughout the day. However, the impersonal nature of a texted message entices some youth and adults alike to venture into inappropriate sexual topics that would never come up in other settings. Many youth have innocently been drawn into texting conversations that turn sexual in nature and become far more explicit than any face to face conversation they might have. This sort of texting is called *sexting*, and includes talking about sex, sexual issues, sending sexually explicit pictures or material through an electronic text message. It is becoming quite common in this age of ever-present technology.

Because it seems so impersonal and detached, some people mistakenly think that there is no harm in sexting. But, there is great harm in sexting. Consider that sexual feelings are aroused during explicit sexual conversations; the sacred nature of sex is usually minimized or ignored when sex is discussed in an impersonal setting; sexting disregards the emotional and spiritual facets of sexuality, and tempts youth and adults alike to focus only on the physical dimension, effectively distorting the beauty of sex. In reality, sexting becomes verbal pornography if only words alone are used, and visual pornography if it includes immodest images.

If parents want to prevent or stop sexting, they will at least need to have appropriate boundaries around the use of cell phones, and regularly monitor what types of communication and what types of friends their children are texting. The relationship parents have carefully nurtured with their children can facilitate such loving checkups, to where youth willingly share this type of information without parents having to pry it from them.

5. *What amount of kissing is appropriate prior to marriage?*

Kissing is a form of affection that can become sexual. When kissing moves from a sincere expression of affection to an inappropriate level of passion, it will weaken the adolescent relationship and diminish personal spirituality. A person can tell if they have crossed this line when physical triggers start to arouse sexual feelings and entice progression toward sexual intercourse. Passionate kissing is one of those triggers. So avoiding the initial sexual arousal is the most successful way to prevent inappropriate physical stimulation. Adolescents need to understand that kissing, touching, hugging or having sexual conversations can trigger their sexual response, which then encourages more sexual escalation. Helping our children understand this pattern of sexual arousal will help them know when kissing is starting to cross the line from affectionate to passionate.

6. *What is appropriate affection?*

This is a thoughtful question that parents should hope they will be asked by their adolescents. Of course this question is better asked *before* the adolescent has done anything they might consider inappropriate. At any rate, the posing of this question creates an ideal atmosphere for a general talk about sexuality. Some topics that could be addressed are the questions from this chapter, or other principles that have been presented in this book. But take care not to be overwhelming. Teach them that healthy sexuality is based on the three facets of sexual wholeness. Parents could emphasize the connection between being sexually whole and spiritually whole; their spiritual sensitivities can warn them of any inappropriate physical activity.

Sophia's case makes for a good example. Sophia was in high school and had a boyfriend, Peter. They kept the rules and even talked to their parents about their relationship. One evening Sophia came to her mom and asked how to know if their affection was appropriate. Sophia's mom kindly asked how their affection made her feel. Her mom then asked if she had done something she thought might be wrong, to which Sophia replied that she hadn't. Even though they kissed on most dates, it wasn't long sessions of passionate kissing. But Sophia still wondered if they were getting too close to acting inappropriately. Sophia's mom commended her for her spiritual sensitivity, so that their affection could be kept within appropriate boundaries and not spoil their relationship. Despite no rules being broken, such adolescents can intuitively know when they are getting too close to dangerous physical involvement. This is yet another reason why it is important to help our children recognize and understand their own stages of sexual arousal, because the best person to determine if affection has crossed the line to arousal is the adolescent themselves.

7. What is necking and petting?

Parents may think the answer to this question should be obvious to everyone. But some adolescents are confused by the dated terms *necking* and *petting*. Even some young adults are not clear; recently one of us was teaching a group of college students when one raised her hand and asked, "Just what exactly is petting? I have heard the word a hundred times, but nobody has ever told me what it is exactly." Many bishops in their talks with the Young Men and Young Women refer to necking and petting and the need to avoid this type of immorality. Despite not understanding these terms, adolescents usually agree that necking and petting are inappropriate behaviors, and commit to not involve themselves in them. But then dating activities the next weekend result in heavy kissing by some adolescents. Are they blatantly ignoring their leaders' counsel?

We want to point out that some terminology has changed, and when older terminology is used it sometimes confuses children. What used to be called necking and petting is now called making out, soul kissing, hooking up, or non-intercourse sex. No matter what term is used, they all describe the same thing: heavy kissing, sometimes accompanied by touching each others bodies—clothed or unclothed—in a way to arouse sexual feelings without having intercourse.

The key point of this question is to remind us that outdated terminology sometimes impedes clear communication. We need to learn the current vernacular, and talk about why certain activities before marriage will interfere with healthy sexual development.

8. Is it all right to hug?

This question hasn't really needed to be addressed until recently. Hugs were once simple gestures of affection with no sexual overtones. And some still are. Too often, however, hugs have become an opportunity for complete body contact. Some youth linger in the hugging embrace, even swaying while body is pressed against body. In some instances hugs can become more passionate than kissing.

Adolescents should be prepared to decide for themselves what is appropriate and what is inappropriate behavior. And they should come to understand *by what* and *how* their own bodies are sexually aroused. Children whose parents teach through careful reasoning, and allow them to start making decisions at an early age, will see the consequences of their own choices, and such meaningful lessons should encourage them to become more responsible adolescents. But as one parent warned his adolescents, "you are not super human." We are all created with certain physical thresholds of sexual arousal, and full body contact usually triggers that physical arousal. And when that or other physical contact awakens sexual feelings, there is a natural cascade of physical and emotional responses which can easily turn into passionate and then orgasmic arousal. So to avoid getting caught in the natural flood of sexual arousal in the first place, prophets continue to warn youth to stay far away from the physical and emotional triggers.

Table 19.1

Talking to Your Child About Sex
A Quick Guide

Recommendations for age appropriate discussions with children about sexuality.

0 – 3 years old: Instill in your child a healthy view of their body. Use correct terms to describe body parts. If children explore their own body and touch themselves, it is a good opportunity to talk about how wonderful their body is and the need to treat it with respect and take care of it. Always teach about their body with an air of joy, not shame. Teach them respect for other people's bodies as well, i.e., don't hit them, appropriate touching, etc.

4 – 7 years old: Answer their questions about their bodies, sex, or where babies come from as simply as possible, but don't give more information than they ask for. Practice making a comfortable, open atmosphere where you are seen as a source of accurate, complete information.

---

8 years old: They are developmentally ready to understand the basic mechanics of sex. They are still young enough that this initial discussion can plant in them a healthy attitude about sexuality before other influences are felt from media, peers or society. Along with the mechanics of sex, also discuss the importance of the spiritual, emotional, and relational aspects of sex. It is ideal to have both parents participate in this conversation. They will see your relationship as a good example as you talk about the emotional and spiritual strength sexuality brings into a marriage. Again, if the environment is relaxed, you will be seen as a safe, accurate source of information about sexuality

8 – 11 years old: Occasional discussions (about every six months) about sexuality, or questions about puberty, can keep communication lines open. Regularly visit with children about sexuality to maintain a comfortable atmosphere where adolescents can safely ask any question and get straightforward, complete information. If they mention that they heard something at school or from friends—you can clarify it; you have the answer or you can get the answer.

12 – 14 years old: Some children will naturally ask questions while others may need encouragement. Either way, it is essential to keep the channels open during these critical teenage years. Children may hear jokes, stories, or words that need to be explained in a safe setting. They will be developing sexual feelings of their own, and need guidance in interpreting these feelings. This is an ideal time to help them understand that these feelings are wonderful, and will help them create a loving relationship in the future.

Talk with them about their own sexual development and arousal, and help them distinguish between appropriate affection and inappropriate sexual arousal during future dating years. Do not avoid frank discussions; be open to talking about issues such as oral sex, noncommittal make outs, pornography, and arousal. Eliminate any awkward feelings from your discussions to reassure them that the topic of sex need not be embarrassing.

Help children develop a balanced, whole person approach to their sexual identity. This will set them up for solid future relationships. Children whose parents discuss sex with them are less likely to involve themselves in premature sexual relationships.

When children begin to feel strong sexual feelings themselves

If the atmosphere is safe, children may feel brave enough to share with you something they have done—which you might consider wrong or sinful, i.e. seeing an inappropriate image; touching themselves in arousing ways; inappropriate thoughts about a person who is attractive; touching another person to arouse them; or other sexual activities with another person, etc. The most important goals are to keep a safe atmosphere, don't label your child as sinful or perverse, and don't make them feel ashamed.

Children rarely need to be told that they are doing something wrong; it is usually something they naturally feel because of the Light of Christ. Encourage them to explore how they felt when they saw or participated in these behaviors, and how it influenced their relationship with the Spirit. They can learn from their own experiences to distinguish good from evil by noticing their closeness or distance from the Spirit—more than from shaming statements from you.

The main sentiments that should be conveyed are that it is wonderful that they have strong sexual feelings; that those feelings can be a blessing to their life; and that it is wonderful that they are willing to talk to you about those feelings. Together you can work towards helping them learn how to control and direct those feelings in ways that increase your child's happiness, instead of creating problems in their relationships.

20

QUESTIONS ABOUT SEXUALITY DURING ENGAGEMENT

Engagement is an exciting and happy time for couples. In fact, some research shows that it is the season where some couples report the highest levels of satisfaction and happiness that their relationship will ever experience! Some of this may be due to unrealistically positive views of one another, but in many ways it is simply enjoyable and exciting to be sharing a great deal of time together, and experiencing new and strong feelings of love. What couples can sometimes forget in this euphoric state is that there are important tasks still to be accomplished before they are ready for marriage. Even though most engagements lead to marriage, some do not; the engagement period is still a necessary time for partners to test out their relationship to see if it really is the one that they want to stick with for the rest of their lives. In fact, for some LDS couples who did not know each other for more than a few months prior to their engagement, this becomes the *primary* period of testing out their relationship to make sure it is viable.

Do couples need to test out the sexual area prior to marriage? In the non-LDS world, many people would probably answer "Yes" to this question. In fact much research shows that a large majority of couples in most developed countries are sexual within a month or two after beginning to date, and live together prior to marriage. Ironically, such early sexual involvement and cohabitation are consistently linked with poorer relationship outcomes—they are not helping couples make better marital decisions. This research confirms the fallacy of the commonly held idea that sexual compatibility should be tested prior to marriage. When people talk about *sexual compatibility*, they are usually implying that a couple should have a full range of sexual encounters with a partner before marriage to determine whether their sexual styles and preferences are compatible. But there is no evidence in the research that shows that testing out sexual behaviors in this way helps either the durability of the relationship, or the likelihood that a couple will have a satisfying sexual relationship. In fact the evidence suggests just the opposite, that those who refrain from being sexual prior to marriage are more likely to stay married, and have better sexual relationships after marriage.

Still, even for conservative couples who refrain from full sexual involvement prior to marriage, there is some degree of testing that does occur in the sexual area, but it is in regard to *sexual attraction* rather than specific sexual behaviors. Sexual attraction is the fuel that drives sexual arousal and involvement throughout marriage, so it is an important element of most satisfying relationships. The level of sexual attraction is something that couples are usually aware of—regardless of whether they have been sexual with one another.

Here are a few questions that are commonly asked by engaged couples that illustrate some of the testing that is necessary in the sexual area:

> *1. I really love my fiancé and we can talk about anything, but I don't find myself very attracted to him physically. He isn't ugly or anything, but there just doesn't seem to be that spark for me. Should I be worried, or will this spark develop over time after we are married?*

> *2. In our relationship I am almost always the initiator of physical contact. We are not sexual and are otherwise doing what is right, but my partner rarely wants to kiss or hug me, and it's not because he thinks these things are wrong, as we have talked about that. We plan to be married in a few months and I'm worried that my partner will still be the same and rarely initiate physical things in our relationship that I think are very important. Is all this an indication of a serious problem?*

> *3. I'm aware that my partner has made some serious mistakes in the sexual area in prior relationships, and I feel that he has properly repented. But I would like to begin our relationship with total honesty, and think it would be good if both of us fully disclosed our pasts and talked about these things. Would this be wise?*

4. It is very hard for us to keep our physical relationship within the proper boundaries. We are so attracted to each other and are very much in love. We are each committed to stay worthy for a temple marriage, but sometimes I still worry that we are too physical, and should be focusing on other things. Will this change after we are married?

5. I must admit that the sexual part of our relationship really scares me. We both feel attracted to each other, but I just don't know what to expect after we are married. I'm worried that my ignorance will cause our honeymoon to be less fulfilling than it should be. I have so many questions, but nobody has ever really talked to us about the sexual part of marriage. Is there a good source where we can go to learn these important things before we get married?

As you can see, many questions are a result of inexperience, and will be answered naturally through the course of marriage. Still, we see that some of the issues that are emerging prior to marriage might significantly influence the quality of their relationship after marriage.

Sexual Attraction

One key aspect that couples may still be testing out is their sexual attraction for one another. Most couples start a relationship because they have at least some level of physical attraction to one another, but some have not evaluated this aspect very closely and may need to carefully consider it. The first and second questions illustrate people who are worried about very disparate levels of physical attraction between partners. Even though there are natural differences in the importance of physical attraction between genders, the concerns mentioned by the couples in the first two questions should be taken seriously. While it is possible that feelings of physical attraction may grow over time, our recommendation is that if this is already a concern, they should delay marriage until they figure out whether there is sufficient physical attraction between them. How strong does it need to be? There is no clear answer to this question, and we acknowledge that physical attraction is only one element of a healthy relationship. But if it doesn't exist prior to marriage, it is not likely to develop much more after marriage.

If the individuals asking these questions are attracted to other people of the opposite sex—but not to their current partner, this is probably a warning sign that this important element may be missing in their current relationship. If, however, the individuals have never felt strongly attracted to anyone of the opposite sex, it may indicate a problem that could use careful evaluation and possibly some therapeutic help.

Sometimes a lack of physical attraction for anyone indicates abnormally low hormone levels, which is often a sign of a serious physical problem. In some cases, if an individual has no strong feelings of attraction for someone of the opposite sex—but they do for someone of the same sex, this may indicate same sex attraction. In other cases, a person may have heard so many negative or guilt-inducing messages about their natural sexual feelings, or they may have experienced sexual trauma such that all of their sexuality may be totally repressed.

Regardless of the source of the problem, marriage is not a solution to problems of attraction. For example, people who have same sex attraction do not suddenly become attracted to the opposite sex just because they get married and become sexual. Likewise, people who have experienced sexual trauma or who have unresolved issues about this do not automatically heal and recover once they get married. Such challenges need to be addressed prior to marriage so that once each partner enters marriage, they will be fully aware of what their issues are in the area of sexual attraction, and can feel confident that there is enough attraction to fuel a healthy sexual relationship. Without a sufficient degree of sexual attraction, it will probably be very challenging for partners to become interested enough—or aroused enough—to have a fulfilling sexual relationship.

Previous Sexual Sins or Problems

The third question deals with the disclosure of past sexual sins. This is a sensitive topic and one with fewer easy answers than some scholars and professors may have implied over the years. Some purport that any sins that have been fully repented of should be left in the past, and not brought up by either partner. This is a principle that can be followed by many partners without causing a problem, but should not be applied dogmatically since each relationship is unique.

There are, however, benefits to having as much openness and honesty in a relationship as possible. And one of the ways we can be open and honest with one another is to discuss our pasts, and evaluate whether past problems have really been overcome, and whether personalities are still able to mesh well. Of course we would expect that if a person, due to previous problems or past experiences before joining the Church, had acquired a sexually transmitted disease, they would disclose this to their partner before marriage. Nevertheless, there are more than physical consequences for people who have been sexual with others outside of marriage—even if they have repented. We regularly hear in church that we are free to choose between right and wrong, but we cannot avoid the consequences of those choices—even if we have repented and have been forgiven. Does a potential spouse deserve to know the consequences of prior sexual behaviors before they make a final decision to marry? In some instances the answer is clearly "Yes."

Each individual, each couple, and each past circumstance is unique, but we recommend that during the later stages of exclusive dating and the early stages of engagement that partners offer information as well as ask questions of each other. If there are hints of previous problems in the sexual area, the decision to ask more about them or disclose them should be handled prayerfully and sensitively. Once the Lord has forgiven us of our sins, He remembers them no more; it is implied that we should try to do the same thing with others also.

Is it necessary, though, to also seek forgiveness from a potential marriage partner for previous serious sins? We believe that our covenants with God—and a future spouse—are violated when individuals are sexual with someone else before marriage. Consider that the future spouse is inadvertently injured—even if the person sinning hasn't met their future spouse yet, and even if they fully repent before they do meet them. Nevertheless, this does not always mean that the future spouse needs to be fully informed about such previous indiscretions or asked for forgiveness, even though in some circumstances this would be appropriate.

If couples keep in mind these facets of the principles of repentance and forgiveness, and at the same time balance them with the important principles of openness and honesty, they should be able to find a solution that fits their unique relationship and personalities, one that will help each of them make the best possible decisions about a future marriage together.

Sexual Restraint

The fourth question we posed at the beginning of this chapter has to do with the ability of individuals or couples to restrain their sexual impulses. Relationships that are overly focused on sexual involvement—before or after marriage—will be weaker than relationships that are more well-rounded, and include closeness in other areas we have discussed previously. There is no season in life where sexual discipline is not needed. Some individuals may naïvely think that once they are married they won't have to worry about sexual restraint ever again. This is clearly not the case. There are more times in a relationship when engaging in sex is not the best thing to do than there are times when sex would be appropriate. In addition to the busyness of normal life, each couple will likely be visited by times of illness, depression, separation due to job demands, pregnancy, etc., all of which may prevent a couple from being sexual as often as they would like.

People who haven't learned how to restrain themselves prior to marriage are likely to have the same challenge restraining themselves when needed after they marry. There is no better time to learn how to have a well-rounded relationship—one that is not overly focused on sex—than prior to marriage. This is the time to develop strong communication skills, to engage in activities and talk about interests that are enjoyable to both partners, and to test out whether there is a sufficiently strong foundation to the relationship that does not include sexual bonding. Sexual bonding can then be added after marriage as an additional aspect that strengthens and builds on this stable foundation.

Sexual Ignorance

The last question is an important one, where someone is worried about their sexual ignorance and the problems this may bring to a relationship. Two primary reasons for our writing this book were to help couples avoid some of the common pitfalls that occur early in marriage in the sexual area, and to compensate for the fact that many people are not given good guidance about sexuality from family or church leaders. We hope that couples will use the principles in this book to help them start—or re-start—better in the sexual area of their personal lives and in their relationships. And the next chapter should be particularly helpful for new marriages. In essence we are writing this book because we believe it is important, if not crucial, for couples to have access to more thorough information about their sexuality before and after marriage. Most couples will look for information about sexuality in one place or another, but it is preferable that they obtain it from trusted sources—including books—that are consistent with their own values, their family ideals, and the teachings of Church leaders.

21

QUESTIONS ABOUT WEDDING PLANS & HONEYMOONS

The wedding day signals a distinct departure from how a couple used to act to how they may now act as a married couple, particularly for those who abstain from sexual intercourse prior to marriage. With the vow to care for each other as husband and wife comes the privilege to elevate the sexual relationship beyond casual expressions of affection like kissing to more complete expressions of sexual intimacy.

Marriage unites two separate people into one unified whole. The powerful symbolism and literal meaning of such a union can hardly be missed. God commanded Adam and Eve: "Therefore shall a man leave his father and mother, and shall cleave unto his wife, and they shall be one flesh" (Genesis 2:24). Sexual union in marriage has a power to strengthen emotional and spiritual bonds. The physical union implies that a couple should also be unified in purpose and methods. Preparing for such complete unity certainly requires maintaining your chastity, but you also need to understand sexuality in marriage in order to have a positive experience on the honeymoon. Some young couples may think that if they have maintained their virtue, they are sufficiently prepared for marriage. Virtue is very important, but naiveté is not a friend. Preparing for intimacy in marriage requires additional information from knowledgeable and trustworthy sources.

Another symbolic meaning of the commandment to be one is in the idea that as a whole number, one cannot be divided by anything but itself. If the two of you are united there is no outside source that can divide your marriage. Becoming one is the lifelong aspiration of marriage. And as we have discussed in previous chapters, sexual unity, spiritual unity, and emotional unity must all be included in developing a complete and wholesome relationship within marriage.

For LDS couples who have deliberately chosen to wait until after marriage to have sex, the honeymoon is their first opportunity to explore together sexually. The decision to delay sex until after marriage carries with it not only important religious implications, but also priceless psychological benefits; studies affirm that couples who abstain from sex until marriage are more likely to reach higher levels of marital satisfaction. This is just one of the many advantages that naturally flow from not having sex prior to marriage.

In sharp contrast to the worldly exploitation of sexuality, within marriage sexuality can be nurturing to both partners and their relationship. Setting clear, healthy patterns at the beginning of your marriage will encourage positive affection. With that in mind, let's discuss specific aspects of sex and the honeymoon that form the basis for many questions and which are appropriate to discuss in a book of this nature.

What is a premarital exam?

A premarital exam is a thorough pelvic exam by a qualified medical provider that is very beneficial for even the healthiest of people. A number of potential problems are looked for, and if discovered can most likely be treated. Additionally, couples can learn things that may add to the success of their marriage, such as a basic review of anatomy and the functions of the reproductive organs.

Choose a medical provider who is willing to take time to thoroughly answer any questions and discuss any concerns. For those who may feel awkward or embarrassed to ask such personal questions, you might consider writing down your questions prior to the appointment. Then when you meet the medical provider, you can simply hand her the paper and she can address each question during the course of your exam.

It is beneficial for the groom to attend as well. After the bride's private physical exam with the health care provider, the groom can join them, where important questions can be addressed such as birth control, the basic functions of the reproductive organs, the mechanics of sex, or any fears or anxieties surrounding sexual intercourse.

A medical provider, however, generally does not offer much practical infor-

be helpful for the couple to talk to someone who can help them prepare for the sexual side of marriage, such as a trusted family member or two—preferably a married couple. If the relationship with parents is healthy, they could be invited to have a detailed discussion with the engaged couple, helping them anticipate what will happen, the process of meeting each other's sexual needs, and typical gender differences such as the importance of the female clitoris in reaching sexual enjoyment for women. This can help ease the transition from virginity to sexual unity. If either one is uncomfortable with this option, the engaged couple may be better served by talking individually with their respective parents or a married sibling. Either way, the wishes of the couple should take precedence— no matter how strong outside opinions may be to the contrary. Men especially can gain insight about female sexual needs by talking with a trusted married friend, and thereby feel less anxious about how to help his new wife enjoy sex. Obviously, if a couple's parents have been tight-lipped, embarrassed, or guilt-inducing about the subject of sexuality in the past, they would not be a good choice to approach for advice.

What if I don't know how to act on my honeymoon?

We hope you will remember that a honeymoon is not about sexual performance as much as it is about the beginnings of sexual exploration, and simply getting to know each other in a more complete way. Sometimes it may be a difficult emotional transition for newly married couples to accept that what was long prohibited is suddenly allowed after the marriage ceremony. It may take some time to adjust and settle this notion in your heart and mind. Many newlyweds have no problem embracing the distinction, and they are anxious to explore what they previously could not explore. No matter which group you find yourselves in, you will be treading in new territory, and some important cautions should be heeded.

You have learned that many of our attitudes about sex are framed by media, the locker room, or family dispositions which may have viewed sexuality as something dirty or shameful. Frankly, it can be difficult to separate what you have seen or heard throughout your life from your current expectations of what a honeymoon should be. Nevertheless, it is vitally important that you leave behind what you have heard or supposed as you begin this new season of life that has sex as a major component to it. Base your sexual expectations on the principles discussed in the beginning chapters of this book.

A successful formula for an enjoyable honeymoon is to focus on three simple things. First, don't take sexual activity faster than you are comfortable with. Second, don't take sexual activity faster than your partner is comfortable with. Third, focus on your spouse's satisfaction and pleasure—not just yours—to the extent that it does not violate either of the first two priorities.

For example, just because the speed limit of a highway changes from 35 MPH to 65 MPH does not mean that you have to suddenly speed up to 65 MPH. You should travel at the slowest speed necessary for each passenger to feel safe and comfortable. The same is true for sex on a honeymoon. Just because the "speed limit" changes from appropriate kissing and hugging before the wedding to being able to have sexual intercourse just after the ceremony does not mean that you promptly do so. Sexual "acceleration" should occur at the slowest rate necessary for both partners to feel comfortable. In fact, moving slower rather than faster has several hidden benefits, one of which is it allows ample time for each of you to revel in new feelings and explore each other's ideas about sexuality. If hurried intercourse is the only goal, however, the couple may miss out on the unforgettable depth of this initial sexual encounter.

Sexual pacing is such an important concept that we bring it up in a number of chapters. Sexual pacing ought to be discussed prior to the wedding so that expectations are clear. Sex is so much more than a physical act; in fact, for many it is more emotional or psychological than physical. Sex unconsciously brings to the surface the most hidden and private emotions of the human heart. As such, it is best to err on the side of making thoughtful progress—rather than the swift completion of a goal—and taking time to feel each level of emotion as you explore together. Your real goal should be *intimacy*—not sexual completion.

Remember also that you are the same person after marriage as you were before. If you felt insecure in your relationship while dating, having sexual intercourse after marriage is not likely to alleviate that insecurity. Nevertheless, talking about your fears and insecurities with your spouse will help your relationship and your emotions, and should thereby improve your sexual life.

So, don't feel overly anxious about the honeymoon. Just be yourself, have fun in the celebration, and try to enjoy the journey; let the rate of acceleration take care of itself as you unselfishly focus on the needs of your spouse.

I'm worried about him [her] seeing me naked. I want to lose a few pounds before the wedding, but I'm so nervous it's hard to diet. What should I do?

As we have previously mentioned, a honeymoon is designed in part to give you time and space to get to know each other sexually. A natural part of this is seeing each other undressed. But that does not mean that you should get undressed on any particular schedule. Again, this is an issue of pacing. As you kiss and touch each other, natural physical responses begin to unfold—something that is just as true now as it was when you were single. Then the counsel was to reign in those responses in order to retard sexual activity; but as a married couple, this spontaneous progression is welcomed as part of your sexual relationship. Physical bodies have an amazing ability to respond to touch, verbal messages, and especially visual images. So as comfort levels allow, you should find that seeing each other naked will be a natural experience and not a dreaded anxiety.

Worrying about your weight at this point is probably counterproductive. Remind yourself that your future spouse is attracted to you *now*, so trying to make radical changes at this point will just add unnecessary stress on your relationship. Besides, these types of worries often come from worldly sources that try to persuade us that we have to have a body that looks a particular way. Whatever your body type or style now is, you can feel confident that it was one of the motivating factors in your spouse's decision to marry you. And their body holds that same type of attraction for you. At the appropriate time and when you both feel comfortable, you will be naked in front of each other and it can be an easy experience. There is no need to devalue this first special experience by feeling that somehow you don't measure up to Hollywood's view of what your body should look like.

If you feel like you need to diet in order to be healthier, then diet. That is a different issue from whether you should diet to be more "presentable" naked in front of your new spouse.

Over time, each of your bodies are going to change anyway. Hopefully, as each spouse matures and bodies naturally morph into aged bodies, your attraction to one another will be the same, meaning it will still be to the whole person—not just their physical bodies. We are initially attracted to our spouses for many reasons beyond the physical, including emotional understanding, common interests, sense of humor, and spiritual ideologies to name a few. If we choose to build a healthy and whole marriage relationship, we will nurture our attraction to each other through the vicissitudes of pregnancy, sickness, changes in physical appearance, or mental health. Marriage is meant to bridge such physical transitions of mortal life with a committed partner who is also striving to build an emotionally deep and spiritually secure relationship.

If your honeymoon is approached with all three key dimensions in mind, you should realize that the few extra pounds you want to shed are not really an issue. More important is feeling unified, and building a long-term relationship that includes emotional security and physical acceptance.

What about birth control?

For LDS couples, it is helpful to read the Church's official position on both birth control and the purpose behind sexual relations:

> *It is the privilege of married couples who are able to bear children to provide mortal bodies for the spirit children of God, whom they are then responsible to nurture and rear. The decision as to how many children to have and when to have them is extremely intimate and private and should be left between the couple and the Lord. Church members should not judge one another in this matter.*
>
> *Married couples should also understand that sexual relations within marriage are divinely approved not only for the purpose of procreation, but also as a way of expressing love and strengthening emotional and spiritual bonds between husband and wife* (LDS Handbook 2: Administering the Church, *21.4.4 second paragraph).*

Note how sex is described as a dual-purpose activity—for procreation and for emotional fulfillment and enjoyment. So it is safe to conclude that there are times when birth control is appropriate, allowing husband and wife to enjoy sex unimpeded by the fear of procreating if they do not want to procreate. This, of course, is a very private matter, and like other important issues in marriage, the decision should be made by the couple using spiritual insights and feelings.

Every couple has unique circumstances and concerns to consider. So it is the couple's decision whether to use birth control, and if so, the method of birth control. The question of whether to use birth control on the honeymoon ought to be decided long before the honeymoon arrives, since certain methods of birth control require more time to be effective than others.

If the couple hopes to have children as soon as possible, however, then there is little need to address the issue of birth control. Having sexual intercourse with the purpose of trying to get pregnant can be an especially meaningful experience. But there most likely will be seasons where sexual intercourse is desired for reasons other than procreation. And once a couple is done having children, sex is entirely for unifying and strengthening a marriage, which includes emotional fulfillment and enjoyment.

Consequently, it is useful to learn the particulars of the different methods of birth control, which include the use of hormones (the pill or patch) and the barrier method (condom, IUD, diaphragm). The least effective methods which have failure rates between 20 and 50 percent are spermicidal foam alone, and periodic abstinence. There are more birth control options designed for women than there are for men. However, the couple should unselfishly discuss who will bear the responsibility and the effects of the differing methods. Such issues should be addressed with healthy goals in mind, thinking of each other's needs, and using spiritual insight.

You will find that there is no perfect method of birth control in marriage. Each has its own benefits and drawbacks. As a couple, you should consult with medical professionals and others who know about the benefits, risks, and potential side effects of each method. And because sex is a key component of marriage, finding a method of birth control that fits your current situation will allow sex to be used properly to promote wholeness and solidarity.

What if intercourse is painful?

Painful intercourse is a common problem for women and can have many causes. First you must know your own body and be able to describe to your health care provider the location and circumstances surrounding your pain. Painful intercourse can be caused by underlying gynecological problems or hormonal imbalances, which your health care provider can also address. Another cause of painful intercourse is insufficient lubrication. If a lubricant is used but the pain persists, you should visit your doctor to rule out any serious problems.

Another cause of insufficient *natural* lubrication is inadequate arousal. By taking more time holding, touching, kissing, and talking, a husband can help his wife become more aroused, and this process can begin long before intercourse—even hours before if you want. Such arousal prepares the woman's body for sexual intercourse. Small gestures meant to stimulate arousal will begin the process of producing lubrication in the woman's body. Chapter 11 addresses the importance of the clitoris in women's arousal and may be helpful for this issue. Remember also that connecting on an emotional and spiritual level can be very stimulating to a woman.

Pacing is a key principle to remember with this problem. Slowing the pace of sexual activity may allow the woman to feel more at ease and accepted, and thereby increase her feelings of trust and closeness. It may be helpful to review the first chapters of this book with this particular issue in mind. You might also consider the following questions: Are you as a couple spiritually close? Can you risk talking about feelings or concerns? Have you created an atmosphere of closeness and trust? Can you let go of the goal of an orgasm for now, and simply enjoy being physically close?

Will I feel guilty after having sex on my honeymoon?

As a standard matter, having sex on your honeymoon is entirely within the scope of what God allows, *unless* doing so runs contrary to one spouses' needs or fears about sex. But if both of you are ready for that kind of encounter, then there should be no reason for guilty feelings. If you have sex just to please your spouse, even though you don't think you're quite ready, that's not something about which you should feel remorseful. However, if you want sex—and your spouse is not ready—and you move ahead anyway without regard to their feelings, then you will have done so for just your own pleasure and not for the benefit of your spouse. We should feel some measure of sorrow and regret when we are calculatedly selfish.

There is a physical and hormonal release or let down after sex which can be misinterpreted as guilt or disappointment; if individuals had orgasms prior to marriage which were caused by individual or couple behaviors, and felt guilty about such experiences, the physical release after sex we are referring to might become associated with earlier feelings of guilt. After having sex in marriage, there is no inherent reason to feel guilty after this sexual climax and release, even if it occurs prematurely compared to where your partner is in their stage of sexual arousal. With time and experience you can learn to pace yourself in ways that are more satisfying to both of you. As discussed in Chapters 6 through 11, the natural buildup toward a climax of orgasm comes down after the orgasmic release; this precipitates a downward plunge in heart rate, hormonal release, and sometimes the euphoric feelings which are also associated with the buildup.

There are sexual complexities and nuances to learn. While the honeymoon is a perfect time to begin this education, the tutoring should continue throughout a healthy marriage. It takes some devotion and work to learn how to share sexual encounters in marriage that are satisfying for both partners. Both spouses should become very conversant about the differences of arousal in men and women, as well as the time required for each to achieve orgasm. But this is an educational process that can be fun and very rewarding—emotionally and physically.

Experimenting with sex for the first time on a honeymoon soon reveals the emotions of sex, whether positive, negative, or a mix of both. It may be painful the first few times you try it, casting a cloud over the experience. And some may have been the victims of abuse prior to their marriage. Prior abuse certainly has the potential to stir up negative feelings when having sex. Others may have been raised to believe that sex is dirty or wrong, a "necessary evil" associated with procreation. Those who suffer from such difficult pasts are at a greater risk for feeling negative emotions after having sex.

Couples who go on their honeymoons in a spirit of humility and with a sincere desire to please their partner should have a positive experience, especially if they try to pace their sexual progress to that of their partner's. Sexual union in marriage is approved by the Lord. It can bring powerful blessings to a committed marriage and a measure of resiliency to a couple as they meet the challenges of family life.

22

QUESTIONS ABOUT SEXUALITY IN MARRIAGE

In this chapter we will address three questions couples often ask us about sexuality in marriage, and we will do this by applying the principles presented in Chapter 16 on Sexual Decision Making.

1. My husband sometimes buys me lingerie he likes and wants me to wear. It is fun to wear and it seems to arouse both of us, but I wonder if it is too "worldly." Is it?

2. We both like oral sex as much or more than intercourse, but a friend once told me something she heard from a bishop that this wasn't natural and shouldn't be practiced by LDS couples. It never bothered me before my friend mentioned this, but now I sometimes feel guilty and wonder if we should only be having "natural" sex instead of oral sex. Should I feel guilty?

3. I have a very difficult time reaching orgasm, and we discovered that the only way I can reach orgasm is if I stimulate my clitoris during intercourse. Am I sinning because I am touching my own genitals, like people do when they masturbate?

Each couple will likely have their own unique sexual practices and fantasies that help them enjoy each other and their bodies. In two of the questions we detect some level of discomfort with these practices. But what is the real source of their discomfort? Some people have heard that whenever a couple doubts whether something is right, it is an indication that it is not right. This can prove to be true in many cases, but by itself, such a feeling is not sufficient rationale for making decisions. We consistently find many people who have guilty feelings about almost everything sexual due to improper sexual conditioning or detrimental messages about sexuality. For such people a feeling of discomfort would likely be a poor guide to what is best for the couple. We also know from research that whenever individuals try anything new or different, many people feel at least some degree of discomfort, and the discomfort is particularly strong in people who do not like change. Again, we can see that some feelings of discomfort may not be related to whether or not something is appropriate.

Additionally, we find situations where one partner feels no discomfort while the other one feels significant uneasiness. Is this because one is more spiritually sensitive than the other? Or are they just too anxious or paranoid about doing something wrong? In our experience, couples are all over the board in regard to these issues, so the first principle we want to reemphasize is that each partner must know themselves well. If they have negative attitudes about sexuality in general, if they have been sexually traumatized, or if they often have a difficult time with anything new or different, then a feeling of discomfort may not be a good primary indicator of whether a certain course is right for their relationship. On the other hand, however, if they are relatively secure with their sexual feelings, and if they are usually comfortable with trying new things, then feelings of discomfort can be trusted; they should pause and carefully consider whether what they are doing—or are contemplating doing—is good for their relationship.

One of the central points in Chapter 16 is the idea that a couple needs to thoughtfully consider whether what they are doing will draw them nearer to each other and nearer to God. This means that any practice that is degrading or that involves people outside of their relationship would be very inappropriate. God has commanded us to maintain strict boundaries around the sacred area of our sexuality, so it is not appropriate for a couple to have any other person involved in that part of their relationship. The only exceptions to this might be when a couple is stuck and unable to progress, or they have such vexing problems that they need outside guidance from their bishop and/or a qualified therapist. Even in these instances, though, a therapist or bishop could be cornered into offering an opinion on a decision that is best made by just the couple.

Notice the second question at the beginning of this chapter and how the individual who shared with a friend, who shared with a bishop, ended up feeling guilty and confused where no such feelings existed beforehand. Is this because oral sex really is wrong? It will now be much more difficult for the person asking the question to figure this out, because while this particular couple had been enjoying this type of sexual activity without guilt, now the idea has been planted in their minds that it might be unnatural. Are their newly found feelings of guilt something that they should trust?

It is difficult to imagine that any bishop would offer an opinion about oral sex unless the couple pointedly asked if this type of behavior was okay. Most of us would be shocked and dismayed, and would consider it an invasion of our privacy, if a bishop asked us to disclose the sexual behaviors we were or were not doing in our marriage. It would be very unusual for a bishop to ask whether a couple was practicing a particular kind of sex. Therefore, this specific counsel likely emerged because the couple or the individual was uncomfortable making their own marital decisions, and so they asked their bishop to do this for them in a round about way. If the individual referred to at the beginning of this chapter had not been divulging her private sexual behaviors with a friend, there may not have been any guilt. But does this mean oral sex is okay as long as the person doesn't feel guilty about it? What it means is that many of our vexing questions about what we should or shouldn't do in marriage in the sexual area are exacerbated by not following the principles in Chapter 16, which includes inviting other people into our sexual relationship that don't belong there.

In nearly all cases, a husband and wife should be the only ones making decisions about sexual practices in their own marriage. It may be that for some couples oral sex is not good for their relationship and for others it is fine. While this may sound relativistic or valueless, again with the exception of a few behaviors mentioned earlier, Church leaders have not issued specific official statements for the general membership on these issues, indicating that it is left up to the couple to decide. If this is truly the case, then one couple might decide that oral sex is something that works in their situation and helps their relationship, whereas another couple might decide that it does not.

We should be grateful for such ambiguity. Even though we might sometimes think that it would be easier if we had a detailed set of rules about marital sexual behavior, if we insisted on depending on such a list from our leaders we would be falling into the trap of the Pharisees in the Bible. The result would be that we would become overly rule-bound by the letter of the law, miss the mark of the spirit of the law, and miss out on the personal growth that comes by making our own decisions.

We will now turn to the question about lingerie to help illustrate these principles. How might our opinion change if the husband, in this instance, wants his wife to wear lingerie every night in place of garments—rather than just as a part of a specific sexual encounter? If the couple agreed to this, they are not honestly evaluating whether such behavior is consistent with the counsel of the Church, because those who were married in the temple have covenanted to wear the garment both night and day. While this does not mean that garments can never be removed for sexual activities, the expectation of wearing garments most of the time is clear.

Since the triangle mentioned in Chapter 16 includes both members of the dyad and God, His expectation should be considered along with that of the couple. If His opinion has not been declared in official scripture or in general conference, we can find it through personal efforts such as prayer and fasting, study, and exercising faith. We must also remember, however, that in many instances the Lord may not answer our prayers in specific and plain ways, which thereby implies, as Elder Richard G. Scott has taught in general conference, that the decision is up to us (see "Learning to Recognize Answers to Prayer," *Ensign*, November 1989). As instructed in the scriptures we should "counsel with the Lord in all of our doings," but sometimes the Lord's answer is simply, "You decide."

From a scientific view, there is no data that indicates that lingerie, oral sex, or self-stimulation during a couple's sexual activities harm marital relationships. Couples can and do participate in many different sexual positions and practices, even though most couples answered on surveys that their previous sexual encounter involved vaginal intercourse. Most couples also answered that their favorite and most common sexual encounter includes vaginal intercourse. The next most common sexual encounter includes oral sex. But such responses do not remove the obligation for couples to make their own decisions about what kind of sexual encounters they may try.

Even though a particular sexual behavior may be common, widely accepted, or backed up by scientific facts, it does not inform the couple very much when they are trying to decide whether such is an appropriate behavior for their relationship. They should talk about what they want to try, experiment, and consider their feelings before, during, and after sexual encounters in their marriage. It is vital that they involve their spiritual self as well as their physical and emotional self when deciding what will be a part of their sexual repertoire.

Most importantly, each couple should take care to not allow their different preferences to drive a wedge between them. If one partner would rather not participate in a particular behavior and reasonable discussion does not resolve this difference, it would never be appropriate to manipulate, coerce, pout, or punish one another until someone gives in. No specific sexual technique is worth driving a wedge between partners and exercising unrighteous dominion. While this may seem simple enough, it is a lifelong endeavor to consistently make decisions that honor the desires of both partners as much as possible—especially when differences in personality and sexual conditioning are thrown into the mix.

23

QUESTIONS ABOUT SEXUALITY ACROSS THE LIFESPAN

One of the more challenging and intriguing aspects of sexuality is that it is a moving target. As humans age their physical bodies change, the circumstances surrounding their relationships change, and their desires and interests also tend to change. Just when a couple feels like they have reached a satisfying sexual plateau, something typically happens to that upsets their equilibrium. For example, a pregnancy, a new job, moving, sickness, losing or gaining weight, etc., are all things that can substantially affect sexual experiences. So there is a regular need to reevaluate and readjust in the sexual area or the couple runs the risk of problems creeping in over time due to neglect. It may be helpful to review Chapter Six on Eroticism, and this chapter will address some additional ideas.

In the normal development of couple intimacy—along with changes that emerge over time, couples grapple with differences in sexual desire, and differences in the need for creativity and variety. Both issues are intricately intertwined. As monotony invades the sexual area, a loss of interest in sex usually follows for one or both partners. Keeping sexual interest and enthusiasm going in the relationship is a challenge for most couples; the demands of life sap our energy and time, hormone levels change, monotony builds up, and creativity wanes. Many readers may be interested in this book primarily because of these very challenges. Perhaps more mature couples are concerned because they have lost the zip and interest they used to have in their romance, or maybe younger couples are struggling to figure out how to meet the stronger sexual interests of one person without making sex distasteful for the other.

It is highly unusual for both partners to consistently want to be sexual on the same days, with the same frequency, and with the same levels of variety. For the rest of the population, it requires that a couple prioritize this important area of their lives, and work to keep their sexual relationship healthy and vibrant. Here are a few of the questions we have heard that indicate couples are having challenges maintaining their sexual relationship over time:

1. Since the birth of our second child about six months ago, our sexual relationship has been pretty poor. We both seem exhausted most of the time and the baby has been very colicky, so it isn't like one person is interested and the other isn't. But should I be worried that we are going to damage our relationship if things don't change soon?

2. My husband complained to me the other day that he thought our sex life was boring. I had to agree that we generally do the same things, but I do like it and we are both orgasmic. He suggested we try a book that would give us some new ideas. I'm not averse to that, but I don't think any of the books he has suggested are appropriate. Can you recommend any sources to help us that don't have pornographic pictures or crass language?

3. I think both of us were very attracted to each other up to a few years ago, but I've noticed that we are letting ourselves go physically. We are both overweight and inactive, and this has affected our sexual relationship. I tried to suggest that we start a diet together but my spouse doesn't seem motivated. What can we do to change?

4. I find that I am not nearly as interested in sex now as I once was. I never dreamed that this could happen because earlier in our marriage I wanted to have sex much more often than my wife. Now it seems that things are reversed, and I'm wondering if that is normal?

Note how each of these questions illustrate how sexual relationships can change over time. Even though none of these couples seem to have a sexual disorder or other serious problem, it should be obvious that what was once fulfilling and enjoyable has become strained and less satisfying. It is likely that every couple will experience similar highs and lows in their marriage. Nevertheless, we want to emphasize at the outset that sexual equilibrium can return—with persistent effort and time.

Here are some of the most common ways couples have coped with these challenges, which we have found both in the professional literature and in the comments we have heard from couples.

How couples cope with decreased interest in sex due to monotony

Couples and professionals suggest several ways to increase variety in sexual relationships. Perhaps the most common is to try different sexual positions. There are countless sex manuals and videos that explicitly show many different ways couples can have sex. Even though they give ideas that may help couples discover a new way to have sex, and maybe even help them break out of a less than satisfying routine, there are several problems with this option. The first problem is that explicit pictures or videos of other people engaged in sex would be considered pornographic by nearly all LDS leaders and members. There are some sources that include more delicate and abstract illustrations of different sex positions that are not likely to be arousing or considered pornographic. But to find tasteful illustrations of this type would likely require wading through inappropriate material and risk being exposed to pornography. The spiritual damage that occurs when viewing sexually explicit material is real and should be deliberately avoided. We would never recommend any such manuals or videos to our own children for their marriages, and we do not recommend any of them to you.

Another problem with this particular approach to ending monotony is that all of the sexual positions can really be boiled down to four primary positions: male-on-top; female-on-top; side-to-side; rear entry; and sexual acts such as oral sex that don't involve intercourse. Each couple can and probably should experiment with these four basic positions and find several that are enjoyable to them. Of course it is to be expected that some encounters may not be particularly fulfilling; it may take several attempts to discover the best angles and positions to fit your particular body styles and preferences. If couples approach such sexual creativity as a fun way to explore and enjoy their bodies—but without a particular outcome in mind such as mutual simultaneous orgasm—this kind of experimentation can become an enjoyable part of their sexual relationship.

Beyond these four basic positions—and nuances within each position, most of the unusual combinations that are presented in books with themes such as *100 Sexual Positions to Try* require extreme dexterity or physical stamina that is beyond everyone except maybe gymnasts or other professional athletes. In other words, most of the sexual positions beyond the basic few are fictional if the real goal is to find a way to experience sex that is satisfying for both partners. One way to add variety, however, could be to occasionally participate in a sexual encounter that is really only very satisfying for one spouse. It may be nice to be pleasured by your partner on occasion without worrying about your partner's needs. But if this is the primary solution to fixing problems of monotony, it will probably be insufficient in the long run.

We find that couples who are frustrated with monotony can easily vary their sexual encounters by experimenting with different positions, locations, and even times to be sexual—if they are willing to put some thought and effort into it. The solution, then, is not so much reading a manual to find a new sexual position as it is in prioritizing their romantic relationship, caring enough about each other to occasionally try something new: get away to a new location, try on a new outfit, talk about sex, tease one another a little bit, and it may surprise you how it can rekindle interest. The feeling that sex is becoming boring is one of the early indications that couples are neglecting their relationship.

The most serious threat in looking for solutions *outside* of your relationship is that there is no such thing as a permanent end to monotony. The new thing couples try may eventually become dull, or the new book may loose its appeal; so a couple may dig up more extreme materials to read or view to get ever new ideas. The spiritual damage that comes from following this detour can be lethal to a relationship; eventually couples or individuals can get so far off track with their compulsion for variety that they are viewing hard core pornography and sharing sex with people outside of their relationship.

The need for variety should always be tempered with the need for propriety, respect, and realistic expectations. An analogy might be helpful here. Some people seek out the excitement or "high" that comes from speed or very challenging physical activities. If they do not carefully bridle such passions, they may eventually find themselves putting their lives at risk by going too fast in a vehicle, or climbing a mountain that is beyond their abilities. Likewise, people can accumulate great debts by spending money they do not have, or waste their time thrill-seeking, all at the detriment of much more worthy causes or the well-being of their family relationships. Such thrill-seeking can turn into compulsions, and should be moderated by appropriate limits on time, money, and safety so that serious mistakes are not made. In much the same way, sexual thrill seeking has similar risks as athletic or other forms of thrill seeking. If the desire for sexual variety is not kept within appropriate boundaries, the damage that may eventually occur to the relationship will be worse than if no variety had been introduced in the first place.

Furthermore, if people were physically active by running only on a treadmill, it would probably be hard to stay interested for the long term, and important muscle groups would be neglected. If an occasional walk outside, a swim, a hike, or a bike ride is introduced, the monotony of the treadmill the rest of the time can be tolerated better, and exercise can be more consistent and beneficial. Similarly, couples can and should find ways to add some variety and creativity to their sexual life, just as they look for variety in other areas of their lives. The unique thing about sex, when it is done well, is that it includes two loving partners who both bring ideas about creativity and variety to the relationship, not leaving it dependent upon the creativity of just one person.

How couples cope with different interest levels in sex

In several chapters of this book the problem of different interest levels in sex between partners has been mentioned. The purpose here is to discuss some of the ways couples cope with this problem, and what may be the advantages or disadvantages of each approach.

The common challenge in this area is that most men desire sex about twice as often as women; but these gender differences are inconsistent, and besides, as couples age it can even reverse where wives desire sex more often than husbands. Regardless of which partner is more or less interested, couples need to develop a strategy to cope with different interest levels in sex.

One of the first things that successful couples do with this particular difference is to normalize it. This means they accept the fact that it is irrational to expect both partners to have the same exact sex drive, and that there is no reason to take this difference personally. This normalization helps couples avoid the otherwise uncomfortable situation where one person indicates an interest in sex and the other one expresses that they are not interested. If they are mature enough to not take this personally, they do not interpret such different levels of interest as a sign that one person isn't a good lover, or that the other person doesn't care. Showing this kind of maturity is the most important first step in managing differences.

Other strategies that couples use to cope with different interest levels include switching back and forth which partner chooses their frequency of sex during a particular week or month; engaging in sexual activities other than intercourse, such as manual stimulation of one partner by the other where the focus is primarily on the partner who is interested; one partner always acquiesces to the desires of the other; both partners try to compromise and focus more on their partner than on themselves; or, one partner participates in solitary sexual activity such as masturbation—with or without the awareness of their spouse.

It should be obvious that each of these options vary in their potential to really help the couple maintain a vibrant and healthy sexual relationship. While we are loathe to suggest which may be the best approaches, solitary sexual activities are not likely to help the couple draw closer together—especially when they are done in secret—even though such may temporarily reduce tension or conflict. We consider that the primary purposes of sexual behaviors are to help couples share physical and emotional closeness that will help them bond and strengthen their relationship, and procreation. This means that coping strategies that involve solitary sexual activity, or require one partner to always give in to the desires of the other are inconsistent with the primary purposes of sex in the first place. A more mature and sensitive approach would be to flexibly manage the differences in sexual interest in such a way that neither partner feels that their wishes are usually ignored, and that neither partner feels that they usually have to give in to manipulation by the other partner.

Let us suppose, then, that one spouse wants to have sex twice as often as the other. First of all, he or she should not feel bad or guilty about this difference. Second, he or she should feel safe expressing their interest level in sex and how attractive their partner is, but such expressions need to be moderated by their knowledge that their spouse has a lower sex drive. So if they have been sexual recently, or it is obvious that tonight is not a good night, it may be best for the interested partner to restrain their sexual interest and not even mention it. Third, the partner with the lower sex drive should on occasion try to think about or do things that help increase their own interest in sex. Sometimes if the reluctant partner thinks about or talks about sex with their spouses, touches, kisses, or hugs them more than they normally would, wears particular clothing, or does other things to help them feel more sensual, they can, happily, become more interested in sex. Fourth, couples can experiment with ways of pleasing just one person that doesn't involve as much time or effort as intercourse. Some couples find that taking a shower together, or massaging the partner where he or she can be aroused to orgasm is a nice way to meet sexual needs without requiring a longer encounter that includes mutual orgasm or intercourse. Fifth, with persistence and practice, and especially with more concern for their partner than for the self, couples can develop a consistent frequency of being sexual that is a *little more* often than the reluctant partner prefers, and a *little less* often than the interested partner prefers, but becomes generally quite satisfying for both of them, and helps each one feel loved and appreciated.

How couples cope with busy lifestyles that crowd out time for sexual intimacy

We have found, and the research supports it, that happy and satisfied couples are generally sexual on a weekly basis. Taking age and certain circumstances into account, this may mean many times a week for younger couples but only once a week or so for older couples. Nevertheless, even though older couples may not experience orgasm as often as younger couples, we find that they are still quite connected physically to one another, and their sexual experiences are often more fulfilling than they were when they were younger.

In other words, couples who prioritize their relationship find a way to consistently be sexual with each other, and when they are not able to do this, it is enough of a concern for them that it is addressed as soon as possible. Some couples schedule sex consistently on the same day, and they are open to additional spontaneous days as they come up, but at least they can anticipate their special day or time that is just for them. Some couples may not need to schedule sex because their lives are not as busy and they have a good track record. Many happy couples also have special times during the year where they escape to enjoy one another away from home. We think the Orthodox Jewish idea that the Sabbath is a day where the Lord expects couples to rest from their labors and enjoy sexual activities as a couple is a wonderful way to keep the romance alive.

24

QUESTIONS ABOUT SEXUAL DISORDERS

Physical and psychological problems that affect the ability to have sex often become the most difficult stumbling blocks to sexual intimacy in part because discussing them can be more awkward and distressing than talking about other sexual issues. Unfortunately, because sex is such a deeply emotional issue, avoiding such physical or psychological problems can make matters worse.

Many marriages have periods when one partner or the other suffers from either a persistent physical or psychological sexual disorder. Ironically, and despite the difficulty, dealing with sexual dysfunction can be an opportunity for growth. It allows spouses to better understand the fears, concerns, and/or anxieties each faces. Each spouse can still try to do their best to satisfy the physical and emotional needs of the other, and this will in turn create a more meaningful depth to their sexual encounters. While some disorders or dysfunctions can be treated with medication or professional therapy, often at least part of the source of the problems can be found within their own relationship. Even if medication is used, couples express greater levels of success if they also address their relational issues surrounding the disorder openly and sensitively.

I don't seem to get aroused as often as my husband. He feels that I am not attracted to him, but I am. I wonder if I have an arousal problem?

Not being aroused as often as your spouse is not cause for alarm on its own, and does not necessarily indicate a lack of attraction to your spouse. Spouses naturally have different arousal levels. You can refer back to Chapters 7–11 for more details on physical arousal and desire; Chapter 11 outlines the specific differences in women's arousal patterns. One often overlooked key to managing sexual differences such as this is to openly express your feelings and concerns with your spouse.

Women's lack of desire or arousal usually centers on a lack of emotional or spiritual connection with their spouse, a necessary ingredient that encourages physical arousal. In this case, your husband has an opportunity to learn from you that you may view sex much differently than he does. Your views on what stimulates desire for sex are not necessarily the same as what may arouse his desire. Bringing these differences out into the open allows you to then work together to change your sexual approach, or how he can better stimulate you not just physically but emotionally as well. You may simply feel exhausted and not have as much energy as he does for sex. So if your husband is made aware of this, he can then help with the children, do the dishes, or give you some alone time. If, however, you feel your desire or arousal problem is more serious than these natural differences, you may need some professional help.

I struggle with premature ejaculation. I want to help my wife achieve orgasm, but I consistently reach orgasm too quickly. What can I do?

This is an admirable question to ask because studies show that nearly 1 in 3 men deal with premature ejaculation at some point in their relationship. We want to point out that both men and women are affected by premature ejaculation. The pressure of not peaking early only adds to a husband's anxiety. Wives, too, can become frustrated if her husband's consistent premature ejaculation signals the end of their sexual encounter and she has yet to reach orgasm.

Consequently, men often find themselves trying to focus on *everything but sex* so that they don't peak too early. But some methods for dealing with premature orgasmic disorders—such as thinking about something else—may not contribute to the long-term health of the sexual relationship. Some may think that premature ejaculation is caused by getting too worked up during sex. However, it is far more likely that men who struggle with this problem are feeling anxiety more because of the heightened emotional intimacy they feel. So in order to power down emotionally, they try to think about other things—but which effectively disengages them from the deeper aspects of the sexual encounter. Premature ejaculation can also be disengaging by creating an escape route from the holistic intimacy of sex. But for those couples who are willing to talk about and work through these usually hidden anxieties, sexual encounters can not only be lengthened but deepened into more meaningful experiences.

If during sex a man is more aware of when he might be disengaging from the full intimacy of sex, and the woman is also aware that her actions and verbal reassurances can be a source of comfort and calm, the man can then begin to let go of his anxieties of intimacy and stay fully engaged in the sexual encounter. We emphasize again that truly intimate sex focuses on pleasing your spouse, not in the pleasure that sex brings you individually. However, we cannot please our spouse if we are wound so tight that we are unable to process genuine intimacy.

Another strategy for dealing with this problem is for a husband to focus his *mental* energies on simply finding ways to please his wife. Focusing on his wife's pleasure can do two things: first, it can arouse his wife more quickly, as she feels that her husband is trying to connect with her both emotionally and physically; second, it is a more effective way to take the husband's mind off of his own arousal.

We have found that yet another useful tool is trying different sexual positions. If the woman is on top she can feel more control and thus greater arousal; the man may feel less stimulation and thus better able to focus on giving his wife pleasure. You should experiment with different positions to find the benefits of each. Additionally, if the male wears a condom this can also forestall ejaculation, since sensations are somewhat muted.

It may be, especially early in the relationship, that focusing on his wife and her arousal will still bring on early orgasm for the husband, even if they are not in the process of intercourse. New sexual encounters are sometimes overwhelmingly exciting, but especially to inexperienced husbands. We underscore that even though one partner reaches orgasm, it should not mean that the sexual encounter has to end, especially if the couple has learned how to continue the process of arousal using ways that do not necessarily involve intercourse. To that end, you may also benefit from the information about sensate focus described in the answer to the following question.

How can "sensate focus" help sexual disorders?

An exercise called *sensate focus* can be very useful in treating premature ejaculation, erectile dysfunction, difficulty lubricating, or difficulty feeling aroused. Initially couples concentrate on the simple sense of touch, without touching breasts or genitals. Orgasm is not the goal. The couple talks out loud during the exercises, discussing how touching and discovering each other's body—without intercourse—is pleasurable. This may be a new world for some couples, or at least remind them of the pleasures of being close to each other without the endgame of intercourse or orgasm. This exercise, especially if practiced at different times, also helps to reduce high levels of anxiety. Relax by hugging, kissing, holding, and expressing emotions, and thus gain a fresh appreciation of how being with each other physically can be a goal in itself.

Once couples are able to feel comfortable with non-arousing touch, they can then begin to experiment with arousing touch, but still not touching breasts or genitals. The goal for these particular exercises is not to cause an erection or lubrication, but instead learn how to calm any anxieties that may be a part of their intimacy or performance. By removing the pressures that are sometimes felt during sex, couples may find that many sexual disorders can resolve themselves just by learning how to relax the sexual environment and slow down the pace.

Again, once the husband and the wife feel comfortable with this level of arousing touch, they can then begin exercises where they do touch each other's genitals and breasts with the goal of causing an erection and lubrication—but not penetration. Using a lubricant, of which there are several kinds, can help increase the pleasure and reduce the friction, especially when touching the clitoris or vagina. Each partner should pay close attention to how their bodies respond, noting when an erection is maintained or lost, and what encourages lubrication. These simple exercises can be very useful not only for newly married couples, but also for couples who are experiencing physical changes due to pregnancy, stress, illness, or age. These are times to slow down and discover the intimate physical response details about each other.

Once the couple feels at ease with this level of touch and arousal, they can then use a lubricant to attempt penetration. Even a less than full erection can penetrate the vagina if the couple approaches it slowly. The mind-set of each partner at this stage should focus on the subtle sensations they are feeling. Take your time; begin with shallow penetration and remain there until you are comfortable and in control. Once both spouses feel at ease, slowly deepen the penetration. If the wife senses that her husband is losing too much erection, she can move her hips just enough to stimulate his penis, but without any inclination to perform more. As long as the exercise is enjoyable, the goal has been reached. There should be no predisposition to perform, only to enjoy the simple pleasures of touching each other's body, and learning about each other's body in a more fully intimate way.

I'm embarrassed to even mention it, but at times I can't get an erection. I really want to enjoy sex and give my wife pleasure but this problem is so frustrating. Is this a serious arousal disorder or can it be fixed?

Husbands who struggle with erection can start to think that they are inadequate lovers and less desirable to their wives. And thinking this way compounds the problem, and they can lose the ability to achieve or maintain an erection long enough to satisfy their spouse. Women can help alleviate this downward spiral by engaging in open, trusting dialogue, and take care that their criticisms or frustration are not compounding the problem. Men who are able to dispel the myth that the presence of erectile dysfunction somehow diminishes their manhood are much more likely to bring it up and discuss it with a spouse or a medical professional.

Because erectile dysfunction is usually physically caused and psychologically worsened, medication can have a tremendous effect in alleviating the problem. Medication can resolve the physical symptoms while the placebo effect can help stop and begin to reverse the mental spiral that erectile dysfunction often causes in men. Talking to your doctor about medication may be a beginning step to help alleviate this problem.

Couples may also find it helpful to reconsider their sexual goals while trying to resolve erectile dysfunction, since they should be able to achieve sexual satisfaction in ways other than intercourse or orgasmic-based encounters. Traditional methods of intercourse and orgasm can be modified to allow for both partners' satisfaction despite the lack of a consistent erection. A resilient wife can be incredibly helpful to her husband as he faces this vexing situation. If her real goal is to foster intimacy, she can show him ways to arouse her without penetration, and reassure him that intercourse, while pleasurable, is not the only route to satisfaction. For example, oral sex allows the wife to reach orgasm even if the husband cannot achieve an erection, and helps him feel that he can still give his wife pleasure. Similarly, husbands can still reach orgasm without an erection by the wife stimulating the penis. With some creativity, both partners can still achieve a measure of sexual satisfaction with or without orgasm or erection.

I regularly experience painful intercourse. Is there anything I can do?

Painful intercourse, also known as dyspareunia, is almost exclusively a female problem. It is very important for women to know their own bodies so that they can describe the exact location and circumstances that cause their pain. Painful intercourse that stems from gynecological problems or hormonal imbalances should be addressed by a health care provider.

The most common cause of painful intercourse, however, is a lack of lubrication. If other causes of the pain have been ruled out and the main culprit appears to be a lack of lubrication, there are several things couples can do to correct the problem. One of the simplest ways to alleviate the problem is to liberally use a lubricant. Additionally, both the husband and the wife may want to reconsider which methods of stimulation work best for the wife; review the discussion on sensate focus, and experiment to find which types of touch are the most arousing to encourage natural lubrication. We want to emphasize that painful intercourse is a couple issue—not just a female issue, despite the fact that it is the woman who feels the direct pain. The most effective approach to resolve this problem begins by addressing the causes and possible solutions as a couple.

25

QUESTIONS ABOUT MARITAL LOYALTY

Healthy marriages are built on the universal bedrock of loyalty and fidelity. But marital unfaithfulness—or infidelity, takes on many shapes. Some are overtly obvious such as sexual infidelity or divulging a marital confidence. We can usually tell what overt infidelity is by the look on our spouse's face when he or she learns of our indiscretion. But marital disloyalty also includes the more subtle and devious things that gradually erode marital trust and loyalty. Such shady actions include telling personal details to friends or family but not sharing the same with our spouse. Even more damaging to the bond between married partners is when emotional ties are formed with a non-spouse—even if they are not sexual.

Even though infidelity or disloyalty can creep into any marriage, it is far more difficult for infidelity to find a toehold if both partners are vigilant and actively trying to stay loyal to their marriage. If we are actively working on our commitment to our spouse, we are less likely to succumb to marriage-eroding behaviors. Healthy marriages require consistent attention and assessment; they are not like flying a plane on autopilot once an established route and altitude are achieved. They are more like driving a sports car down a winding mountain road, exhilarating and challenging—and subject to devastating consequences if the driver takes his or her eye off the road for more than a few seconds.

Because marital loyalty is affected by many different situations, and because disloyalty can sneak in and overwhelm couples, we want to discuss some important questions about marital loyalty using the principles outlined earlier.

Is viewing pornography disloyal?

The short answer is *absolutely yes*. But why? To answer the question we need to examine how viewing pornography measures up to the four principles of healthy sexual relationships that we discuss in this book.

Principle #1: Does [the act of viewing pornography] draw us closer to each other and God?

Research confirms what modern prophets have proclaimed, that pornography negatively affects marriage. Research also shows that there is a significant reduction in a couple's emotional connection if pornography is used within the marriage. So, even for couples who feel that pornography is acceptable if viewed together, they should be aware of the detrimental effects it will surely have on their emotional and spiritual relationship. Clinical studies bear out that even though pornography causes an increased desire for sex, it also diminishes emotional connections. Any sexual conduct that does not foster emotional and spiritual strength is detrimental to a marital relationship. Because pornography focuses on just physical arousal, emotional and spiritual aspects of our natures are left unnourished.

Pornography separates sexuality from the whole person and the whole relationship. It creates a sexual experience that is self-focused, and does not nurture the attachments to a spouse for a holistic, healthy sexual relationship. The delicate skills of affection, authenticity, communication, and responsiveness are left underdeveloped and weakened by pornography use.

Principle #2: Does the couple agree about this aspect of their marriage?

In most cases, pornography is viewed privately or secretly by one spouse, not together as a couple. And because of the secretive use of pornography, it means that one partner is engaging in sexual experiences with which the other partner not only does not agree, but likely doesn't even know are occurring. This seriously erodes trust between the marriage partners. Furthermore, such a condition begins to traumatize the non-viewing spouse in many ways. The wife, if it is the husband who is viewing pornography, may sense that the atmosphere has shifted and that her marriage is struggling, even though she has yet to clearly identify the main source of the trouble.

Principle #3: Does [viewing pornography] reflect a positive and healthy attitude about sexuality?

A vital ingredient of sexual health is based on the principle of exclusivity. Pornography violates such exclusivity by inviting images or written descriptions of people outside the marriage into the couple's private sexual relationship. It makes no difference whether pornography is viewed as a couple or individually. It is difficult, if not impossible, to maintain a genuinely intimate relationship if it is regularly infiltrated by toxic outside sources.

Principle #4: Does this foster the sexual needs of my spouse and myself?

No long-term need is met by pornography. It promotes the dark doctrine of detached and selfish sexuality, not connected and selfless sexuality. That it increases physical desire may be true, but the price is paid by a decrease in emotional and spiritual connections and belonging. The doctrine of the soul, however, teaches that our physical and spiritual needs are interconnected and inseparable—opinions of men to the contrary notwithstanding.

If pornography use comes to light in your marriage, it is important to closely examine your relationship and see what marital issues may need to be resolved. The spouse who is drawn to pornography can examine what attracts him or her to pornography. Rare use might be overcome by reconfirming commitments to each other, candidly discussing the problem of pornography, and addressing other concerns individually and within the relationship.

Those who view pornography almost always feel deep shame for their actions. While viewing pornography is terribly wrong, with great effort and outside help it is a surmountable problem. Full disclosure and frank discussions to the spouse and to Church leaders will likely be very difficult at first for both partners. But the seed of hope is planted from full disclosure.

We have been strongly warned by prophets and other Church leaders to avoid the powerful evils of pornography. Gladly, even entrenched addiction to pornography can eventually be conquered, and healing and recovery can replace discouragement and despair. There are four essential components for healing and recovery from an addiction to pornography: spiritual help from a bishop; emotional help from a qualified sexual therapist; regular attendance at 12-Step group meetings; and deliberate personal study. More often than not, the affected spouse will need similar help in order to heal from the trauma she has experienced (see *SALifeline.org* for more details).

What are emotional affairs?

Men and women almost constantly interact with each other in many situations such as at work, church, and social gatherings. When Jan began her friendship with her new co-worker Eric, she was happy to have the association. Eric was friendly and helped ease her transition to the demands of her new job. Although Jan's marriage to Kyle appeared to be fine, she longed for deeper emotional connections with him. In the mean time, Jan and her new friend Eric started to confide in each other about their personal stresses at work—and soon enough about their personal frustrations at home. Interestingly, Jan began to feel less concern about her lack of connection with her husband because she now felt that her need to emotionally connect was being better met by her friend Eric. She soon believed that her lack of emotional connectedness with Kyle was Kyle's problem, not hers.

Sarah and Will had been friends in high school. Years later Will found Sarah on Facebook, and they started to keep track of each other through their updates; eventually they began sending messages and emails to each other more frequently. Although Sarah and Will were happily married, the time they spent chatting on Facebook concerned their spouses. Sarah got irritated by her husband Jon's pointed questions about this "friendship," and she even divulged this to Will.

Casey loved his wife, Julia. He also enjoyed hanging out with the guys. Before Casey and Julia were married, Casey golfed nearly every weekend with his friends, and watched whatever college games were on TV. He started to sense that Julia was not happy about the inordinate amount of time he spent with his buddies, but because she did not bring it up in any conversation, he decided to just continue to ignore the sticky issue. It wasn't long before he began to share his personal successes and stresses more with his friends rather than with his wife Julia.

What are the common threads in each of these examples? There are a number of similarities. To begin with, one spouse has allowed emotional distance to creep into their marriage, and has invited people from outside the marriage to share increased feelings of emotional closeness. Such are *emotional affairs*, and diminish the exclusivity of a marriage relationship. They have allowed someone other than their own spouse to fill their emotional needs, or with whom they can share triumphs, sorrows, concerns, or frustrations. These people may even try to blame the loss of emotional connection on their spouses, or as a result of being bored with the relationship. Even though maintaining healthy friendships outside of your marriage is appropriate and important, once anyone outside of the marriage takes preeminence over the spouse in terms of emotional and physical closeness, a key boundary has been crossed and is inappropriate.

Diminished exclusivity is almost a package deal, as it can then bring diminished communication, trust, responsiveness and authenticity. Even if the spouses may still be talking to one another, the sharing of emotional or physical connections with anyone outside of their marriage will obstruct true intimacy within the marriage.

Lastly, at least one spouse in each example is not proactively trying to nurture their marital relationship. The most potent inoculation against the threat of emotional or physical infidelity is to repeatedly strengthen your relationship. Some useful questions to help you gauge the health of your relationship are: *Can you frankly talk about sensitive feelings and issues? Can you openly and maturely address feelings of jealousy, disappointment, or loneliness? Do you talk about important and meaningful experiences? Do you express your positive feelings about your spouse, and regularly reaffirm your commitment to the relationship?*

Emotional affairs usually begin quite innocently. Still, if the healthy principles of sexuality are regularly reviewed in your mind and strengthened in your couple relationship, the subtle yet harmful effects of emotional affairs can be avoided.

Can sexual affairs be overcome?

The short answer is a resounding *Yes!* However, the short answer requires a long process. Overcoming sexual affairs requires a unique commitment from both spouses in order to repair a very damaged relationship and create a healthy, whole relationship. Issues of trust, commitment, loyalty, belonging and even the very premise of the relationship need to be reevaluated and then reestablished for healing attitudes to prevail over the long term. For some this is not a possibility given the complexity of the situation. For others this is an option that can help rebuild, renew, strengthen, and add maturity to the relationship that wasn't part of the original marital equation.

When a sexual affair occurs, it is a somber omen that the couple has serious intimacy problems that have gone unacknowledged or unaddressed. You may recall from Chapter Four that mature intimacy isn't afraid to address negative aspects of the relationship as well as positive aspects. Some people feel that they must divorce their spouse in order to heal from such egregious betrayal, but for others healing can occur while staying *with* your spouse. It is important to distinguish between healing and forgiveness versus the viability of the relationship. Healing and forgiveness are personal issues, and are essential for individuals to recover and go on to live a satisfying life. The viability of the relationship, however, depends on whether both partners are willing to fully commit to the relationship, and address all the issues that caused the affair and have emerged since the affair. If one or both partners are not fully committed to the relationship and embrace the changes that need to occur, then the process of healing and forgiveness may need to take place after the relationship ends. It is possible that if the proven path to full healing and recovery is religiously followed, and given sufficient time, a couple in these circumstances may eventually be able to reach higher levels of true intimacy than they had before.

Once the problem issues are clearly addressed and acknowledged, instead of attacking each other, many couples start to heal and recover. The power of the atonement of Jesus Christ can repair damaged hearts, trust can be slowly earned back, and loyalty can be painstakingly reestablished.

Clear boundaries for both spouses must be established and maintained in order for a more healthy relationship to emerge. Sexual principles need to be carefully reviewed and applied. Sexual intimacy may need to be reevaluated or withheld for a time until a measure of trust is reestablished in the foundations of the relationship.

With either an affair or an addiction to pornography, each partner will need to seek help from a qualified therapist. Such outside help needs to coincide with the consistent efforts and studies of the couple together as well as individually. Reestablishing trust and open communication will take great effort and patience. The process of forgiveness usually takes time and cannot be rushed.

After a breach of loyalty, how do you ever trust and fully give yourself sexually again?

A marriage is not something that should be easily discarded, despite what our worldly culture may espouse. Because of the deep commitment LDS members feel toward marriage, this particular question takes on added significance. Love is given freely, but trust is earned. And earning back trust after a breach of loyalty takes time and skillful work from both spouses.

When an egregious breach of loyalty such as a sexual affair occurs in a marriage, both parties are permanently changed. Even if repentance is sincere and total forgiveness is extended, the couple is a different couple. This change can either be for better or worse. Understanding what caused your spouse to make such drastic choices can be an influential experience that teaches both spouses to be more vigilant and nurture their relationship more carefully in the future. It can highlight personal weaknesses and strengths. On the other hand, it can also trigger poignant feelings of guardedness or closure that make it extra hard to reestablish a truly intimate relationship.

What happens in your marriage is significantly affected by the skills and maturity of each spouse. Building sexual wholeness in marriage is more difficult than anyone may want to imagine. But the institution of marriage, like a family, is also a first-rate laboratory that helps people grow. Whether the problems in your marriage stem from gross infidelity or simple ineptness, if you are willing to confront yourself and your spouse about the sticky issues, and kindly and persistently work for their solution, this sets you apart as a mature partner.

Addressing issues of loyalty with the sexual principles in mind will help each partner to analyze where improvements should be made, and how choices can be made more wisely. Establishing a healthier sexual relationship can add to the healing process of forgiveness within the marriage.

Are sexual fantasies a sign of infidelity?

If sexual fantasies include thoughts or images of a person other than your spouse, the exclusivity of your marriage relationship is violated—much like it is when one spouse views pornography. Neither does fantasizing about someone other than your spouse pass the four principles of a healthy relationship which we have discussed at length. Sexual thoughts about someone besides your own spouse may arouse you, but such unhealthy arousal harms the relationship, erodes spiritual dynamics, and weakens the emotional well being of both spouses. Poets, prophets, and the Savior himself remind us that seemingly innocent thoughts are really the seeds of behavior. If such fantasies are entertained, the stability of the relationship is on a slippery slope.

As [a man] thinketh in his heart, so is he (Proverbs 23:7).

Sow a thought and you reap an action; sow an act and you reap a habit; sow a habit and you reap a character; sow a character and you reap a destiny (Ralph Waldo Emerson).

Whosover looketh on a woman to lust after her hath committed adultery with her already in his heart (Matthew 5:28).

Instead, when immodest thoughts of someone other than your own spouse come to mind as they occasionally may, a quick dismissal by replacing it with a more noble thought is the most useful approach. Again, consistent and focused efforts to maintain and improve a healthy marital relationship are the best defense against moral entropy. If we are actively showing our unconditional loyalty to our spouse, we are less prone to succumb to cunning marriage-eroding behaviors such as fantasies about others.

26

Conclusions

We have covered a wide breadth of issues and questions in this book, but as we complete our work together it has become clear to us that for most of the topics we have only been able to scratch the surface. We have tried to focus on central issues, key principles, and common examples that illustrate problems and how those problems might be resolved. Of necessity we have avoided making exhaustive lists and unnecessary explicitness. Even so, we imagine that there still may be some who, after reading this material, will feel like we have been too explicit or have given too much detail about such a private and sacred subject. We apologize for any deficiencies, and affirm that we have not intended to be offensive or crass about a subject we ourselves consider so sacred and central to mortality and our salvation. One of the more difficult challenges in writing this book has been in finding that narrow sweet spot of balance where we are lucid enough so as to not be misunderstood, yet not so explicit that we become vulgar or tawdry. We hope we have struck an appropriate balance for our readers, and solicit your feedback about how we might improve upon it in the future.

With that sincere epilogue, may we return to the beginning. Sex and salvation are intricately intertwined. We hope this book has helped you see this truth in a new light, and has provided you with a hopeful message about how our sexual encounters in life can lead us toward greater unity with each other and with God. Our marriage relationships and our bodies truly are miraculous, and there should be precious few days where each of us do not fall on our knees and give thanks for these two supernal gifts. It is only within these relationships of permanent commitment where we are allowed by the Lord to fully express and enjoy our bodies.

A number of years ago a wise Jewish Rabbi mentioned that in his view *sin* was when we did not appreciate nor enjoy the blessings that God has given us. This definition of sin may be particularly true of sexual relations. Most of us have been taught that sin in the sexual area is when we think or do things beyond the limits that have been set by the Lord. While we agree that knowing and staying within these fixed boundaries is crucial, we hope we have opened your eyes to the possibilities for virtuous sexual wholeness that are well within those strict boundaries.

We want to share 10 guidelines that should foster an appreciation for your spouse and your marriage:

> *1. Give daily gratitude to God for the gift of a soul, and all the wonders that come to us because we can touch and feel and share physical and spiritual feelings that lead to oneness.*
>
> *2. Enjoy the image of God after which you were made; see this image in your spouse and children; and teach them to worship a God who has given you wonderful sexual capacities that draw you toward your spouse and enable you to have children.*
>
> *3. Take the name of your spouse, and everything that this represents, into your heart.*
>
> *4. Keep your sexual relationship holy; reserve weekly times for you and your spouse to enjoy sexual oneness; don't allow your sexual relations to be contaminated by any unholy encounters.*
>
> *5. Honor your roles as father or mother by teaching your children to respect and appreciate their bodies, and to develop healthy sexual attitudes.*
>
> *6. Celebrate and nurture your divinely appointed sexual passions with your spouse; do not smother your eroticism through neglect or feelings of shame and guilt.*

7. Cleave unto your spouse emotionally, spiritually, and physically and unto none else.

8. Hold sacred the time you have with your spouse on earth by not squandering it on frivolous activities, technological distractions, or pursuits that do not keep your spouse and family in a place of preeminence.

9. Pursue a life of full authenticity in the sexual area of your relationship.

10. Enjoy and appreciate whatever degree of sexual closeness you may have in your relationship; build on this with hope and faith; don't focus on your own or your spouse's deficits.

We finish this book by expressing our deeply held conviction of the potential for every relationship to become whole in the sexual area. We do not have these convictions because we ourselves are whole. Rather we hold them because of sacred moments with our spouses which have pierced the mortal veil of incompleteness and allowed us to touch a bit of heaven. On those serendipitous occasions we have tasted—even if only fleetingly—the overwhelming joy that comes when our bodies, minds, and spirits feel completely healed and whole. These sacred experiences, though rare, have confirmed that the reward of everlasting oneness is well worth enduring the vicissitudes of this life. Let us all nurture our spouses and children back to our heavenly home where we can be united with our Heavenly Parents because of the Great Plan of Happiness and the atonement of our Elder Brother, Jesus Christ.